I'M JUST NOT HAPPY

# RHODES TO SUCCESS

Other Books By CAROL L. RHODES, PH.D.

Why Women and Men Don't Get Along
With Norman S. Goldner, PH.D.

Affairs: Emergency Tactics

# I'M JUST NOT HAPPY

## SEVEN SECRETS TO RELATIONSHIP HAPPINESS

HOW TO ELEVATE VAGUE THOUGHTS AND
FEELINGS OF UNHAPPINESS TO
CONSCIOUSNESS, TURN A COMMUNICATION
PIT INTO SUCCESSFUL CONNECTING,
REWIRE DEFENSES AND CLARIFY
PERSONALITY DISORDERS

CAROL L. RHODES, PH.D.

Somerset Publishing
Rochester Hills, MI

Published by Somerset Publishing
3585 Warwick Dr.
Rochester Hills, MI.  48309

Orders@TheRelationshipsite.com

Library of Congress Catalog Number:2007902515

Library of Congress Cataloging-in-Publication Data:

Rhodes, Carol L.
    I'm just not happy:
    Seven secrets to relationship happiness

    1. Relationship issues: psychology. 2. Communication barriers. 3. Defensive styles. 4. Personality problems.

ISBN 978-1-4243-3552-7

Bibliography

Cover Design: C.O. & Co.

# AUTHOR'S NOTE

# ACKNOWLEDGMENTS

THANK YOU, THANK YOU, THANK YOU

EDITORS: Norman Goldner, Michael McIrvin, Carol Jonson

COMPUTER
GENIUS: Jason Balinski

READERS: Sandra Palmer, Colleen Rhodes, William Rhodes, Kimberly Papst

# CONTENTS

# INTRODUCTION

Remember those happy days when you felt content and satisfied with life? You may even have had spikes of great pleasure and joy. Then slowly, sometimes traumatically, discontent and discomfort tipped the scales toward much more unhappiness than contentment. You cycled through feeling sad, lethargic, discontented and occasionally, you were down right miserable. It was then that you realized that you were just not happy.

*I'm Just Not Happy* lays out a plan to pinpoint the source of your troubles and then specifies how to resolve baffling relationship difficulties. When anger, verbal abuse, arguments and emotional estrangement leave you distraught, you need not suffer interminably. *I'm Just Not Happy* provides answers.

## UP AGAINST THE WALL

You want or need something from the relationship that is not forthcoming and it may seem that there are no prospects for getting what you need. You've tried repeatedly and in a variety of ways to get better results but nothing seems to work. Things get worse, not better. Then your choices are:

1. Continue to think the same thoughts that produce unhappiness.

2. Learn to endure, give up your dreams and live an angst- filled relationship (perhaps for the children).

3. Leave the relationship.

4. Or, refine your understanding of yourself, your mate, your situation and utilize new methods for reaching your goals.

I recommend the latter. Take charge of your unhappiness through the action oriented methods that are revealed in the following chapters. Practice these techniques and your relationship will either improve or be exposed for what it truly is—irremediable. The following is a brief summary of the organization of the book:


## SECTION ONE

The scope and nature of difficult relationships are contained in this section. To start you out with a graphic illustration of what goes wrong, Chapter One is devoted to the story of a 47-year, problem-filled marriage where the wife finally gives up and hopes that a divorce will stop the pain. Instead, as you will see, she is in danger of leaping from one difficult situation to another—and unnecessarily so.

Chapters Two through Seven also utilize true-life scenarios involving anger, emotional abuse, Internet deceit and adultery as both causes and symptoms of decimated relationships. Immediate and long-term solutions are detailed.


## SECTION TWO

Chapters Eight, Nine and Ten outline defensive styles that heavily contribute to unhappiness. More case scenarios bring to light how perplexing, inadequate and destructive defenses further erode marriages.

## SECTION THREE

Section Three is an explanation of unhappiness caused by complaints, criticism, sarcasm or contempt - communication styles that are the beginning of the end of the relationship. Chapters Eleven and Twelve examine true life stories that reveal how these four factors promote and exacerbate unhappiness and, more importantly, how these issues can be altered or reversed.

## SECTION FOUR

When you live with problem personality characteristics like distortion, dissociation or personalization you are swallowed up in a confusing communication pit. Chapters Thirteen through Fifteen examine in detail the traits of these difficult personalities with specific suggestions to alter each situation.

## SECTION FIVE

Section Five provides a GPS (ground positioning satellite) to restore and enhance your relationship with a step-by-step path to happiness: The Seven Secrets of Relationship Success, The Action Plan.

# SECTION ONE

## Anger, Verbal Abuse, Affairs, Internet Secrets

Chapter One: The story of an unusual 47-year, problem-filled marriage that seemed to have solved itself but, instead, may have gone from the frying pan to the fire!

Chapter Two: If anger is your partner's solution to problems in the marriage, the situation is not hopeless and you are not helpless. This chapter details spousal anger and reveals both short- and long-term solutions. Chapter Three also deals with anger—your own—as well as solutions.

Chapter Four: When faced with verbal abuse you become vigilant and fearful. Chapter Four explains the inner workings of the abuser and how you can manage living with or moving out of the situation. Chapter Five focuses on the inability to leave the verbal abuser.

Chapter Six: This chapter produces a grid to walk through Internet deceit and confront the "innocent Interneter."

Chapter Seven: Issues of adultery are explored in a long-term marriage and what action to take when you feel suspicious, confused and do not know where to turn.

# CHAPTER ONE:

# I'M JUST NOT HAPPY...I WANT OUT

## HAPPINESS IN A LETTER

A phone number I did not recognize appeared repeatedly on my office caller ID two or three times a day for a week. No message was left.

Replying to another message from a former client, Anna, solved the mystery: "My mother, Cara, would like to talk to you. So if it's all right, I'll call her right now and tell her you'll answer the phone. She's been trying to reach you."

Two minutes after I had spoken to Anna, Cara phoned and we set up a counseling appointment. She also made sure I understood that, although she had a phone at home, if I needed to communicate with her for any reason, I had to call her daughter.

## CARA'S AWAKENING

Cara, 68, sashayed into my office for her first appointment a few days later: diminutive (4'10"), with white-streaked brown hair worn straight and short, no makeup, and a nondescript dress and red jacket that looked two sizes too big. Most notable was the sandal on her right foot and a hospital shoe on the left.

Cara explained that she had just had a procedure on her foot and some other elective surgery, but "nothing serious, except that my surgery was scheduled for the day of the power blackout. Luckily, I was taken care of minutes before the lights went out and the hospital went into emergency mode: no air conditioning and dim lights.

"But let's get down to business."

Cara clarified her dilemma and why she had chosen me to help her explore some "sticky" issues. "I wanted to talk to you because my daughter had great success when she came to see you, and I need to talk to someone to figure out if I'm thinking straight.

"I decided to leave my husband, Luke, in March. We've been married 47 years. He knows nothing about my leaving and that's why I didn't want you to call my house.

"I've talked to all six of my kids about getting a divorce. Well, they aren't kids, but you know what I mean. And they aren't shocked that I'm leaving because they know how he is.

"Luke doesn't talk to me, and I mean that seriously. He almost never speaks and when he occasionally has to talk, he lies. Luke lies about everything, even things that are totally stupid. He'll lie about what he had for lunch or if he worked. He's in business for himself and I'm the bookkeeper, so of course, I have to bill for his services and he lies to me about that. How dumb is that?

"Not only that, but he's never been one to do anything with me. He doesn't even go to church with me. He orders me around, and I admit, I follow his orders.

"He ran around on me the first 10 years of our marriage. We were dirt poor and instead of bringing money home for our four stair-step babies, he spent it on himself and other women. He even traded in our poor old beat-up car for a motorcycle. What do you think of that?

"And even now, when I went to the hospital for my foot, Luke didn't come. He said he forgot.

"I've thought about leaving him through the years but last April was the final straw when Luke's brother came to town and stayed with us.

"While they were talking—and I'm sitting in the room with them but they don't talk to me—Luke's brother, Jim, said, 'Luke, you were rotten when you were young.' Whoa, my ears just perked up, and then Luke says, 'Yeah, I don't know how Cara put up with me.' They went on and on talking about the awful stuff Luke did.

"I was just dumbfounded. Luke had never told me he was sorry, and now it seemed like he was proud of all he'd done that hurt me so. Later I told him I wanted to talk. He said, 'Nope, no talk.' That's how he talks to me. I don't think we've ever had a conversation more than two sentences long.

"But, anyway, that's when I decided, 'I'm out of here.'

"Now, this is the other thing that happened. I work part-time in the school office and in May a friend from work called to say a letter had come to the school addressed to me. I told her to read it to me. She said, 'No, it looks like a personal letter.' I thought it was from a school association that always wants donations and I said, 'Go ahead, open it and read it.'

"Well, she did, and I practically passed out. The letter was from a guy I went with for three years before I married Luke. He asked in the note if I could ever forgive him and asked if I'd call him. Well, of course, I called him. I had always wished I had married him instead of Luke because he was such a nice guy.

"Anyway, we got together for lunch. He lives up North, so his son drove him down. I don't know if he was too excited to drive himself or thought he'd get lost or what.

"But, anyway, I'm in love and I'm leaving Luke. I've seen an attorney and he says the divorce shouldn't take more than two months.

"Everyone says I deserve happiness after all these years. My sister even told me to go for it. What do you think of that?"

I think Cara may be jumping from the frying pan to the fire. After 47 years Cara and Luke's relationship problems had calcified to the point that almost any other option would be attractive. Cara was using therapy to sooth and satisfy her children, to avoid blame and to give them the impression that she had done everything possible before leaving their father.

The emotional experience of falling in love feels so good and so right that sound judgment usually goes out the window, and as we can see, for Cara, falling in love meant action, the solution to a 47-year-old problem.

This was an unusual therapy case because Cara had actually solved the problem before calling for counseling. Since she had lived for many years in a state of profound unhappiness this marriage may have been one that could not be saved because her husband was rigid and disinterested in a real relationship and Cara lacked the resources to pull out sooner.

The last I heard of Cara she had left her husband and moved up North, far from her children, grandchildren and friends. Is she living happily ever after? I hope so.

Finding the solution to relationship problems can be daunting. While it is true that when one person changes, the dynamics of the family change, it does not follow that the results save or enhance the marriage. When both parties make a dedicated effort to improve their interactions, the success rate climbs. But, as you will see in this book, if one person makes the right moves, the likelihood of a better marriage goes up.

Avoid being Cara-like, stagnating in a relationship until it falls of its own weight. Do not pass the point of no return. When you read on and take the steps specified in this volume, help is on the way.

## UNHAPPINESS

Unhappiness can be an insidious, low-level form of depression that slyly dances into your relationship in the form of bad behavior, emotional stress or poor communication.

Initially, a problem occurs between you and your partner: over-the-top anger, nasty words, criticism or questionable behavior. You try various solutions that are marginal, work temporarily, and instead of solving the problem, bad behavior and confusing communication spread like a virus.

Suddenly you realize unhappiness permeates your life. You cannot stamp it out. Unhappiness is no longer a simple spike into consciousness or a one-time event; it is a chronic condition.

While unhappiness was slipping and sliding into your life, you became an expert adapter. You adapted to your partner's unacceptable behavior or ugly words by making excuses like, "Her boss is impossible," or "He's on edge because he works too many hours."

Now is the time to be real. Avoid being Cara-like, stagnating in a relationship until it falls of its own weight. Don't pass the *Point of No Return*.

## MIND-SET

Your happiness or unhappiness in life, this moment and every moment, is dependent upon your mindset. Thoughts are things, things that influence and direct relationships in a positive, negative or neutral manner. When relationship thoughts are sour, bitter, angry or even bland, unhappiness exhausts your physical and mental system. Your mind is like a war zone where an occasional white flag is flown but the war is never over.

Relationship understandings often begin in childhood and, regardless of adult reality, childish thoughts, like weeds, are always lurking under the surface, ready to pop up unexpectedly to interpret people and situations as truth. Since historical thoughts do not come to mind as, "Oh yeah, that's not what I think, that is what my dad said," it is difficult to use the intellect to stare them down and stamp them out.

## MIND MASTER

There is an Asian proverb that states, "The mind makes a wonderful servant, but a terrible master." Your mind masters you when habitual feelings of unhappiness piggyback on one another and, just like crayfish fall back into the "miserable" pot before they reach the light of day.

We depend upon habits, old automatic thoughts, to move us from the bed to the job and back home. Every day the physical machinery of our body is on automatic while the mind churns, chugs and sometimes limps along in a conscious, unconscious mode. Signals from the body break into consciousness and send us to the bathroom, the kitchen, or to check the clock while circadian rhythm puts us to sleep and wakes us up. We also depend upon mind habits to define the tenor of our intimate relationship.

For example, if your mind offers up a thought, "Last night, why did Jerry say, 'You should know better'?" The mind as your unhappy master piggybacks that thought with another, "That makes me mad. He embarrassed me and he knew it. He does that a lot and he isn't sorry. I'm not speaking to him tonight and I'm certainly not interested in being romantic." In this case you are your unhappy mind's servant. Your mind offers you a familiar disturbed thought, you accept it as real, add adjectives, emotions and ratchet up unhappiness by several notches.

You are the mind-master when you pinpoint the problem and then take action. "I'm going to give Jerry a call and ask if he is free to talk for 10 minutes tonight.

That's when I will point out that I felt embarrassed when he said, 'I should know better.' If he denies my feelings I will…. If he turns my words against me I will…. If he acknowledges how I feel, we will dialogue and I will feel better." In this case you are the master of your mind.

## FEELINGS

Thoughts also determine feelings. In a new situation your brain can lock the situation and the feeling together. For example, you felt anxious and decided, "I am a poor test-taker." Why? You said something like this to yourself, "Oh no, what if I don't know the answer. If I can't answer the questions I'll flunk and everyone will know I'm dumb." Every time you took a test and had negative thoughts you reinforced exactly what you did not want—a poor outcome. Soon the thought disappeared and you simply experienced the anxious feeling.

Because of our thought habits we often act and react like automatons. We spontaneously move into a feeling state where we either talk to ourselves about how we feel and take it as a fact, e.g., "I feel so depressed" or avoid our negative feelings, shut down our emotions and push them out by denying any difficulty.

We interpret both our emotions and our observation of others' emotions with an inner dialogue. We wake up and feel tired and grumpy. Our inner dialogue then becomes: "I can't get up and face another day. Why is Ron whistling in the bathroom? He knows that irritates me." And the agitation then takes over.

Agitation, if not resolved, will metamorphose into anger, which we explore in the next chapter.

## CHAPTER TWO

# I'M JUST NOT HAPPY...I LIVE WITH ANGER

### THE SECRET OF DEALING WITH YOUR PARTNER'S ANGER

You are not happy with your marriage. Good. Take those unhappy feelings seriously. If your leg breaks you don't drag it around, ignore the pain and assume healing will naturally occur. You immediately call your doctor, go to the emergency room, and take whatever actions are necessary to have the bone reset and properly cared for. Your thinking is focused on solving the problem.

Conversely, when you are unhappy in your marriage, feeling angry, hurt or disappointed, what comes to mind is seldom, "What action should I take?" You may not even think of your distress or the quarrel as a problem because it is a recurring event. Instead, you naturally react with nature's primitive solution, fight (anger and rage), flight (shut down and turn away) or freeze, meanwhile holding your partner responsible for your unhappiness.

If anger is your partner's solution to problems in the marriage you may feel powerless but the situation is not hopeless and you are not helpless.

### ANGER

Anger, according to *Webster's New World Dictionary*, is a "feeling of displeasure resulting from injury, mistreatment, opposition and usually shows itself in a desire to fight back at the supposed cause of this feeling."

*Supposed* is the operative word in this definition since your partner's rage usually springs up without any reasonable rationale and takes you by surprise. You are not happy with good reason if you live with an angry person.

Your partner's anger is bubbling under the surface waiting for an opportunity, a word, a look, a situation, to spew venom in its myriad forms: hysterical anger, bitter anger, sarcastic anger, nasty, or mean spirited anger. Living with an angry person is like living with a mean, stupid drama queen who won't shut up.

Confusion reigns in your mind. You talk to your spouse about your problem with his anger but change does not occur or you may be afraid to mention anger because it's like poking a stick at a gorilla. The anger either frightens you into submission, peace is your goal, or the rationale of your angry partner makes some sort of sense, i.e., "You are too sensitive" or "I am simply expressing my feelings" or "I'm over it. What's wrong with you?" or, in the most common scenario, there is no acknowledgement of inappropriate behavior.

Feeling anger and expressing the fact that you feel angry with an issue is one thing. Abusive in-your-face anger that disgorges sarcasm or slices your character into bits is another. Slicing as in, "You are disgusting. You are a rotten father. You can't do anything right. I don't know why I married you."

You know how to live with unhappiness, you are used to it, an expert at it. Living without your angry spouse may be worse. An anger bully wears you down and eventually the situation feels hopeless but instead of lying down and playing dead, here is a better idea. Use a business model to clarify and alter angry, emotionally charged interactions as Erin and Jason did, the couple whose story follows.

## ERIN & JASON

In an intimate relationship anger is palpable and can be picked up without words through nuances in the face, body language and tone of voice. You become the target of any one of a variety of baby crankiness: sullen or withdrawn behavior, bad-tempered words or, in the worst case scenario, bubbling, boiling anger.

Some people acknowledge their anger but the tendency for individuals is to deny their anger, making others responsible. "You make me mad!" In effect, you should not act or speak the way you do because *you* are the inflammatory agent, igniting my anger.

Erin and Jason point the finger of anger responsibility at one another. They had worked on their unhappy marriage in the past and had altered their habitual sharp words and behavior but found rage creeping back, slowly and insidiously corroding the relationship once again.

In my office for a repeat counseling session Jason, 40, does not so much sit as slumps into the couch in my office, like a sulky child. Erin, Jason's 39-year-old wife, makes a face while she pushes her hair back. They are body experts at conveying their exasperation and ill temper through meaningful looks and subtle movements.

## JASON

Jason is chunky, average height with dark curly hair. He is wearing clothes that have a thrown together as he runs-out-the-door look. Professionally, he teaches seminars. He is a speaker who tours the country with an entourage of energized up-beat people, advising companies and individuals about how to keep their lives on positive, productive paths.

In abstract work settings and with strangers, Jason's passionate, intense feelings are positively focused. He is in charge. In the intimacy of his family he cannot figure out how to be productive and instead is cranky, loud and angry.

Jason reports that Erin's constant talk drives him crazy; after 17 years of marriage he still responds to her chatter with aggravation. In his mind Erin is responsible for their bickering and arguments.

## ERIN

Erin is about 5'5", blonde, dressed in jeans and has long manicured nails, and quick, nervous mannerisms. Erin has a flower business but is primarily at home caring for their 12-year-old daughter and 15-year-old son.

Erin states that she is unhappy in the marriage because "Jason never listens to me. He always acts likes he's mad at me and the children."

Opposition in all arenas is their passion and pleasure, although both deny it. Parenting, decorating their home, spending money, and going to their cottage are all opportunities to argue. You can imagine the emotional chaos generated at home by these two.

Erin begins, "Our problem this time began when Jason refused to stop fighting in front of the children." Jason interrupts saying, "For Pete's sake Erin, the kids can hear us wherever we are. The way you screech everyone within a five mile radius knows every one of our problems."

At this point I remind them that criticizing one another is digging their hole of unhappiness deeper and is not acceptable in my office. Also, I can only listen to one person at a time and since we are here to solve problems, not to fight, let's allow each person their own reality without negative commentary.

Jason sits back semi-relaxed as Erin continues, "Anyway, as I was saying," with a stern look at Jason, "our fighting is vicious and upsets me so much that we don't have good times. We used to at least have good times between the bad times. For months it's been all bad times.

"I feel lonely, angry, frustrated and I don't feel like I'm married or that we're companions. I've tried everything to win Jason over, to no avail. Jason doesn't like me. That's the bottom line."

Jason is silent.

I wait and then, "Jason, it sounds like Erin's been miserable. How are you feeling?"

Jason says, "How do you think I feel?"

I responded, "Unless you tell me I don't know."

Jason concedes, "Well, there is nothing I can do to please Erin. She is always comparing us to someone. Our house is always in process, painting, wallpapering, something, because Erin can't be satisfied. Most of all she's not satisfied with me. Nothing is ever done, solved or finished.

"If I say white, she says black. If I try to suggest a solution she says I'm controlling or bossing her. I am irritable on my way home from the office anticipating trouble."

Jason is ready for battle when he walks in the door. Whatever message Erin wants to convey is lost when Jason sees her expression and interprets it as a reprimand. He then viscerally responds as his system floods with emotions and around they go.

What do you do with a spouse who: (Jason)
1. Screams and yells, uses profanity
2. Is always on edge

What do you do with a spouse who: (Erin)
1. Has to talk; follows her spouse around saying the same thing over and over
2. Is easily upset

Active minds ideally enhance life and marriage. In Erin and Jason's case active minds are used as detonating devices, watching and waiting for the first wrong step.

Their minds are at war in a marital mine field and the first word is the lob of a grenade.

**IMMEDIATE PROBLEM:** Thought patterns in Erin and Jason's marriage are calcified. Erin and Jason have gotten into a daily bickering contest and view one another as opponents. Each declares that their communication style is unlivable, blames the other and refuses to see their participation in misery.

**IMMEDIATE SOLUTION, JASON:** What do you want?

Jason: Peace.

Me: In that case break the cycle of attack-attack. You stop. If you desire peace, you know it is up to you to give up your automatic response. You feel like shouting and yelling. So what? Sometimes you feel like yelling at a customer. Do you? No. You have control of yourself.

The idea that you have to respond with anger is simply the powerful feeling you have when you scream and tension is released. But, after the fact, that expression of anger did not serve you and does not solve your problem.

Here is what to do. Your thinking job is simple. First, do not under any circumstances express your anger. Go upstairs, go downstairs on your treadmill, go outside, and take any action away from the anger scene. Second, respect any point of view Erin espouses and respond by simply acknowledging that her idea has been heard.

You know that it is possible for you to say to Erin, "I understand." If you feel you have to respond tit for tat, go into another room, go outside and walk or run around. Go to the computer and write a story about the situation and what you want and expect from yourself. Do not jump in with another idea or solution even if you think it is positive.

**IMMEDIATE SOLUTION, ERIN:** What do you want?

Erin: I want Jason to control his anger.

Me: You know you cannot control another person. Right? Your job is to manage yourself if Jason is angry. Stick with one thought. For example, when Jason is angry, even though you may feel the surge of old, agitated thoughts and feelings, calm yourself. Here is your response, "I understand."

Erin: Well, I shouldn't have to manage myself because he is out of control.

Me: Right. I agree. You should not but, at the same time, you want to solve this problem. Imagine that forever more he will be an angry person and you have to live with him. What do you do? You decide how to react calmly. If he verbalizes an issue with you, remember that your defenses will jump into place and defenses exacerbate the problem. Bypass your own defenses and listen to him. Acknowledge whatever he says as though he is telling you a story. Think to yourself, "He has a right to his opinion" or any calming thought.

Take charge of the situation by taking charge of yourself. Even before his anger surfaces, before any confrontation, rehearse your response. Do not act on the forceful thought that prompts your defenses. These are old habits, automatic words that do not promote peace.

**LONG TERM SOLUTION** for both Erin and Jason: You are not the judge and jury of your partner's thoughts and feelings. Nuances in the face and body language send messages. Conscious control of negative facial and body language is critical. Stay neutral: no sneers, contorted faces, head swiveling, eye rolling.

1. Quit trying to change your partner. Change is up to your partner's discretion.
2. Stop impulsive reactions including voice tone.
3. Stay focused on what you want in the marriage, not what you do not like or do not want.

4. Continuously remind yourself of what you want. You desire happiness and tranquility. How can you get what you want? Think about solving yourself-problems, not your partner's.
5. You are responsible for your happiness. You are not a victim.
6. You can terminate the marriage at any time; you have chosen not to.

If you cannot think of happiness for yourselves, remember that a war zone is unhealthy for children. Both children have told you that your fighting upsets them.

Once we began marriage counseling Erin and Jason struggled to make changes, eliminate mean words, and show love and affection. They have not separated, have not divorced and appear to have a powerful need to be together as evidenced by their continuous stabs at marriage counseling.

Erin and Jason report that the fighting has stopped which is a huge improvement. They are a couple that need occasional marriage counseling sessions to reestablish and remind them selves of their marital goals. One counseling session every six months has been helpful to keep them on track.

## TRAIN THE BRAIN

An invisible machine located in the brain called the mind runs your life via your thoughts. You are the mechanic in charge of the motor that activates your brain.

1. Your brain is the motor.
2. Attention and purpose are the fuel.
3. Your mind is the driver.

As the driver you are in charge but how do you direct your mind to both immediately handle anger and ultimately solve the anger problem?

Your job after your natural startle reflex response in the face of anger is to get control of your mind. Depersonalize by thinking to yourself that you are watching and listening to a drama, totally unrelated to you and ridiculous, as well. Or, exit quickly when you hear the tone, recognize the look, the body language or the words.

Training is simple; sticking with your plan is hard because the natural mind tendency is to continuously cycle the anger problem instead of focusing on cycling anger solutions. The following are possible solutions:

1. Assume that your partner's angry behavior is written in stone.
2. Given that fact, figure out how to live with anger without disturbing yourself. For example, you are not disturbed by obvious facts, like brown eyes.
3. When you are different, your partner cannot remain the same.
4. View your partner as a baby having a temper tantrum.

You have a concrete choice, leave the relationship, or a perspective choice, change your thinking. If you choose to live with the angry person and desire happiness, the perspective choice is to depersonalize, i.e., keep in mind the anger has nothing to do with you even though the anger talk and feelings are aimed at you. The problem is within your angry partner.

Chapter Three looks at the destructive generational web of unacceptable anger and develops a plan of positive action.

## CHAPTER THREE

# I'M JUST NOT HAPPY...MY PARTNER DOES NOT UNDERSTAND THAT ANGER IS NATURAL

### UNACCEPTABLE ANGER

Anger is a natural and necessary human emotion. Anger can be informative, a personal emotional tool that gives you immediate feedback when you are faced with unacceptable situations, or anger can be a tool used like an wild animal's snarl and growl that generates fear and silence.

1. Anger is unacceptable when anger's emotional force frightens others.
2. Anger is unacceptable when it is used to manipulate and control.
3. Anger is unacceptable when it seemingly jumps from nowhere and is out of proportion to the situation or issue at hand.
4. Anger is unacceptable when abuse is the motive.

One rationalization for acting out anger is that feelings take over and are not under the control of the angry person. After screaming, shouting and verbally attacking you, your partner walks away and expects you to wipe the experience away like spilled milk. She says something like, "Hey, I'm expressing my feelings. You're making it a big deal. What's wrong with you?"

In that case anger is emotional tyranny. Instead of getting a point across or clarifying an issue, the insult and fear generated by anger dominates the interaction.

Have you noticed that an angry person does not care how you respond? Instead, she says, "There you go again. You don't understand, you make matters worse, you twist everything around." In other words, you are to blame and you are responsible. Venomously vilifying you is her right and you are supposed to shut up and take it.

After you have been lacerated by your partner's anger, you psychologically pick yourself up and wonder, "What was all that about?" You, your words or your behavior, have nothing to do with her rage. The actual source of ongoing anger is buried historical, personal pain, learned behavior or a personality disorder that is temporarily relieved by malicious looks, words, tone and action. The squealing rage you experience is a short-term fix while the disturbance that rumbles under the surface is unremitting. Expressing anger simply reinforces the habit and exacerbates the need for tension relief.

But, there is more at stake than momentary rage.

## After Effect

Anger not only has a powerful, negative psychological impact, anger is also physiologically damaging. Scientists have found that the anger expresser and the recipient take hours to return to baseline physiological functions after an angry outburst. The system stays on alert for danger, fearful of the ego assault, anticipating but never knowing when the battering will occur.

Anticipating and managing your partner's anger undermines your immune system and puts you at risk for a multitude of viral and bacterial infections, intestinal disruptions, indigestion, headaches and generally lowers the body's natural resistance to harm.

A 2005 study of couples bickering vs. couples in peaceful relationships indicates that healing takes longer when psychological stress is experienced. A superficial cut placed on a marital participant's hand by researchers healed quickly when a couple was in harmony, twice as long when the relationship was fractious. In fact, it may seem far-fetched but some scientists believe negative emotional experiences bring on, as well as exacerbate, heart problems, cancer, or any chronic illness.

Anger tentacles not only contaminate partners but also stretch across generations. Fathers or mothers whose angry explosions manage the household create fear, damage the marital relationship and teach children how feelings are handled. You don't talk about how you feel; instead you scream and yell.

If you were brought up in an angry family, real feelings and issues were not discussed. You learned to be vigilant and that means you must tiptoe around, fearful that if you talk about real thoughts or real feelings the anger bomb will burst.

The bomb went off too many times in Pat's family.

## THE ANGRY WIFE

Whenever we focus on difficulties in our marriage most of us have particular ways of thinking about and then reacting to issues, responses that may not serve us well. An angry partner will retreat to established dysfunctional reactions, blow things out of proportion and focus on negative aspects of the relationship: Clear thinking goes down the tube.

Pat is an example of anger gone awry.

## PAT

After years of anger directed at her husband, Pat found her marriage teetering on the brink of divorce. Pat had never viewed her anger as a problem. She simply, "Got things off her chest," but when her husband told her he refused to listen to another angry outburst and wanted a divorce, Pat was dumbfounded.

When Pat called my office she said, "I need to see you right away. My husband says he wants a divorce." When Pat arrived for her first therapy session she told me she knew she "occasionally" got angry but she felt helpless to change and, besides, "Doesn't every marriage have arguments?" This is a mind trick. Instead of acknowledging that her husband's experience with her anger is intolerable, Pat is dismissing his feelings. The implication is that he can't take it; he is overly sensitive or doesn't understand the nature of relationships.

Some minds, like Pat's, are a leaf caught in the wind as thoughts race into consciousness and are given credence without consideration—particularly negative emotional thoughts. Pat's mind is filled with angry scrambled thoughts about her husband. Her conscious mind tells her she loves her husband, Jim, and wants the marriage but as though a mysterious force takes over she declares she cannot "help" her negative thoughts and angry outbursts.

Pat's marriage began peacefully because, luckily, when Pat first married she and her husband immediately moved out West, away from her contentious, mean-spirited family. They had an opportunity to establish a relationship focused on one another and, Pat reports, "Those were the happiest times of my life."

After seven years in California Jim was transferred back to Michigan. The move back to Michigan and interacting with Pat's family of origin began the slippery slide into marital misery.

## PAT: THE ANGRY FAMILY

Pat walked into my office, introduced herself and began her first therapy session by cavalierly stating that, "My husband is done with our marriage. He says, 'It's over. Fini.' He can no longer handle my behavior toward him." Tall, blonde, and poised; Pat is a 39-year-old housewife, married for 18 years to Jim, 43, an automotive engineer.

As she speaks about the end of her marriage I do not detect distress. It's as though she's talking about a fictional character.

With eyes glued on me, speaking in a whispery, confidential voice, Pat then shifts from her marriage and begins to ask me questions about my life. I assume the questions are a way to allay her anxiety. Once I change the focus and ask her to tell me about herself she states, "I always view the glass as half full rather than half empty, in fact, I hope some day to be a motivational speaker."

That was the ying, here's the yang. Pat came to therapy because, although she sees herself as a positive person, paradoxically, at every opportunity Pat tears down her husband and says, "I don't know why I do it. The loathing just flows out."

Pat states that she expresses love and affection with her children. She builds up her children's self esteem but she seethes with anger toward Jim.

Where does all her agitation and anger come from? Pat tells me her parents have been separated, not divorced, for 15 years because of vicious, nasty arguments. Her five siblings are pessimistic, moody and put one another down at every opportunity in a "jolly" fashion. (Can people put one another down in a "jolly" fashion? I don't think so.) Pat sees her family style; she says she knows better than to repeat it. She knows Jim is not the horrible person she attacks. She knows her behavior is not justified but she cannot help herself. In other words, patterned family behavior has Pat in its grip.

Pat transfers those early fears to her husband and repeats her parents' behavior. Pat's fear has many octopus-like arms. She grew up without security. The passion of her parents' anger, their threats toward one another of desertion and divorce, physical damage, financial ruin and swipes at one another's core personality were horrific.

Experiences with authoritative parents who turned on Pat and siblings with anger or sarcasm have left open wounds. Pat reports feeling frightened as a little girl listening to her parents fight. When her husband, Jim, talks to her in an authoritative style Pat becomes the fearful child again. Each time she lashes out and silences Jim her experience of power-over is re-enforced. Pat feels satisfaction and thinks to herself, "I was right. I have to let him know how I feel. He can't get away with talking to me like that!"

That is the comforting message Pat gives herself which keeps her impaled on her own petard. This historical retreat is something psychologists call transference. When Pat treats her husband as the enemy, she is transferring feelings she has toward others in the past to her husband. She has identified with the aggressors, her parents, by becoming critical and sarcastic. Instead of feeling emotionally vulnerable as she did as a child Pat has turned her fear into rage and uses it to terrorize her husband.

Out-of-control anger is a habit. Because she is on historical automatic pilot and has stopped paying attention to what she is doing or how Jim is responding, Pat fails to notice the ultimate bad results and, in fact, justifies them.

When a particular behavior is reinforced, it persists. When it is not reinforced, it eventually ceases to exist. In this case Pat is reinforcing the pattern with herself-dialogue ("I have to tell him how I feel!") and satisfaction when her husband appears powerless in the face of her rage.

In therapy Pat indicates that she wants her marriage and wants to change but I wonder:

1. Is she self-reflective? In other words can she stand back and look at her thoughts, words and behavior?
2. Can she control her angry attitude?

3. Is Pat willing to experiment?

The answer is yes, yes and yes but as we know words are easier said than done. In therapy it is important to assess whether Pat is able to acknowledge that her emotional hurricanes are a result of childhood defenses meant to ward off fear, feeling defenseless, criticized and ignored. Secondly, can she understand that she is reacting to her own self-dialogue? And thirdly, is she motivated to change?

Pat's personality style is intense and passionate, so of course her words to herself inflame her. Some of the least noxious words she says to herself, "I can't stand Jim when he looks at me like that. Why would he say that? How stupid! He's deliberately goading me."

Pat said that when she is angry and expresses her feelings she feels good, in fact, great. Her rage feels justified. In other words Pat is exhilarated by her negative passion, her "rightness" reinforced. Although her intellect may suggest to her that expressed anger is a problem, Pat's primitive, emotional self does not want to let go and give up momentary pleasure to face the fear.

Help was on the way as Pat watched her sons' angry behavior. Pat had indicated all was love/love when she was parenting her sons but, naturally, Pat's two sons mimicked their mother's rage when they were upset. Large, teenage boys expressing anger can be scary.

Instead of reacting to her sons' anger with irate indignation, I suggested that Pat view her sons' anger as a visual of her own out-of-control emotions.

When Pat was able to step back objectively and look at herself through her sons' eyes, she saw ugly behavior. And, since Pat was already on her way to understanding that her anger was fear based and historical, the visual seemed to help shift angry thought patterns. When Pat felt the surge of anger she used the One-Minute Rule to immediately alter thoughts and feelings.

## ONE-MINUTE RULE

The One-Minute Rule is a powerful technique for immediate thought rerouting while you get yourself under control. Stop whatever you are thinking for one minute (check your watch), take three deep breaths and say to yourself, "I feel calm." After a few calming words you'll notice your mind wanting to dart away into old thoughts. That is not a problem; you toss out the diversionary thought and immediately repeat, "I am calm." You will feel the calming effect after one minute. Be patient because it takes 40 repetitions to fill up a minute.

**IMMEDIATE PROBLEM:** Controlling Pat's anger habit. She is addicted to the emotional high she experiences with the expression of anger.

**IMMEDIATE SOLUTION:** Because anger is felt does not mean it has to be vented. When Pat is flooded with anger she is to use the One-Minute Rule and then muffle herself for 10 minutes. The point is to stop, think about her thoughts, and take control of what is going on in her mind.

Feelings originate from a thought. What is that thought? Sit down with it. Is it real or is it a flash from the past? Has Jim just done something that is offensive? If so, spitting out hateful words does not solve the problem. He simply feels and hears the poison. Calm your mind and decide how to talk to him. If it is a real problem you can really talk in a normal tone.

1. If the thoughts are habit driven, stop them and decide whether you want to entertain them. If not, redirect thoughts. For one minute, set the timer, say to yourself, "I love Jim" or "Jim is my friend" and totally focus on the words.

2. Change your physiology for 10 minutes or longer: Immediately take physical action. Take a deep breath, cut the grass, take a walk, run around the block, do floor exercises, jumping jacks or jump rope. Physical activity calms the system and elevates the mind. Luckily, as a homemaker Pat is in a position to take immediate action.

3. Another option is to write 10 times: "I feel calm, I am calm." Later, if anger continues to rumble in her consciousness Pat is to practice talking to Jim in a modulated voice about herself, her feelings, or her experience. She is not to say one word about Jim. Pat must carry a small notebook and pencil around and write down thoughts that come to mind about Jim.

The idea is to immediately use any and every method to alter habitual thoughts and to establish a new mental pathway.

## LONG TERM SOLUTION:

1. Where did these feelings and reactions originate? Are they relevant and get you what you want in life? The thoughts and feelings in Pat's psyche may be real but, like an infection, need to be healed through understanding the conflict and by eliminating the repetition of the transference.
2. Institute workable long-term behavioral change. Stop, think, and do not spit out nastiness. Nastiness begets nastiness. The idea that Pat cannot help herself is bogus; it is simply an excuse to say whatever comes to mind with the implication that, "My thoughts are superior and correct."
3. Regurgitating any thought that comes to mind is ridiculous. A question for serious consideration: Do you get what you want when you are nasty? If Pat

replies, "Yes, I get distance. I do not have to interact with my husband and I get rid of the tension inside. I feel powerful." In that case Pat, take yourself seriously and quit acting like your thoughts mean anything about Jim. Those feelings are all about you.

4. Feeling angry is a green light. I am right, you are wrong. I have a right to say anything to you because I am angry and you made me angry. I am powerful when I spew anger. You are demolished; my ego goes up, yours goes down.

5. Positive modeling and being a good mother go hand in hand. Pat had already made strides away from her genetic family modeling with loving behavior toward her children. But, children are sponges. Pat's children undoubtedly experienced fear when she expressed rage toward their father and learned to manage themselves with anger. Since children learn at every age, Pat can help her sons learn new behavior now by altering her actions toward her husband.

## JIM

Jim, Pat's husband, came to a session several months into Pat's therapy and said the person he married 25 years ago seemed to be back. He also indicated, "I am happy and the household is peaceful" but he did not trust that what he was seeing and hearing with Pat would continue.

Now Jim and I had some work to do. Jim felt he had finally taken charge when he told Pat he was done and wanted a divorce.

When Pat eliminated her angry style Jim was naturally fearful that she would do a one-eighty back once he accepted her proclamation that she had changed. I felt his fears were natural but would contaminate the positive strides in their relationship.

**DEALING WITH AN ANGRY PERSON:** Jim had learned a variety of techniques to handle Pat's anger. None of them solved the problem.

1. Jim the authority: "You are a frustrated housewife. You could not survive without me."
2. Jim the psychologist: "Do you understand the psychological damage to your sons when you scream?"
3. Jim the boss: "You are not to say or do that again."
4. Jim the victim: "There you go again."
5. Jim feeding the past: "Well, you are acting just like your father."

The point in Jim's therapy was to alert him to habitual thoughts that produced words and behavior antithetical to his desire for a happy relationship. Thought vigilance is necessary or old thoughts naturally fall into place and contaminate goals.

Consciously living in the moment means grabbing old thoughts and tossing them. Old thoughts are like chewing on gristle. Just chew, chew, chew as though you liked gristle and it was nutritional. It is not and neither is chewing on old, habitual thoughts.

Six months after therapy ended Pat and Jim reported a huge improvement in their life together. Since the addictive nature of the pull from the past is profound, Pat, Jim and I plan to keep in touch to stay on a positive track and examine any new issues that may arise.

**WHAT DRIVES HABITUAL ANGRY THINKING?**

Angry relationship thinking has a life of its own developed in childhood when thought is linear, literal and learning means repetition. Relationship learning takes place as a child observes behavior, listens to words, and absorbs the emotional climate of adult interactions or lack thereof.

This daily imprinting establishes a relationship model in the brain where:

1. You learned relationship confusion. You were unable to make sense out of your parents' interactions.
2. Your relationship thoughts do not include problem solving.
3. A hint of conflict and your brain shuts down, fear filled emotions take over.
4. A hint of conflict and anger shoots through your system.

Each of the above issues provides an unconscious angry current that can chronically interpret life for you. You have established a thought pathway in your brain and then, as a creature of habit, you act and react according to the pattern you have imprinted—good or bad. And why wouldn't you? Are you born knowing how to express your loving self? Are you taught to think and solve personal and interpersonal emotionally laden problems? Seldom, or, given the list above, more likely, never. Anger is the simple, thoughtless solution.

## REPITITIOUS THOUGHTS

Every time a thought or re-lived memory is passed from brain cell to brain cell, a biochemical electromagnetic pathway is established and every time you repeat an angry thought resistance is reduced, just like making a path through the forest. The more you repeat anger to yourself the probability of repetition becomes greater and greater.

## THOUGHT DEFINITION

A thought, as defined by *Webster's New World Dictionary*, is an act of thinking, reflection, meditation or cogitation. Our thoughts conceive, judge, consider, believe, surmise, expect, resolve and work out. We also use thoughts to arrive at conclusions, make decisions, draw inferences, reflect, reason, recall and discover. Reading this definition, thinking would seem to be a monumental task—and, yet, thinking is like falling off a log, simple.

Thinking is both simple and complex. You have 60,000 thoughts a day. A majority of those thoughts will not dock in your mind as they are simply passing through. Some thoughts pop into mind and are necessary for maneuvering through your day, "Oops, yellow light." Some thoughts are innocuous, "It feels like spring." Other thoughts are historically formed and proceed through your mind as emotionalized dialogue, "John sounds just like my dad. He thinks he knows everything."

Regardless of the nature of the thought, whether the thoughts are peaceful, angry or somewhere in between, you are in charge of what stays in your mind to enhance or distress life.

## SCIENTISTS PROVE THE BRAIN CAN BE TRAINED

Jeffrey M. Schwartz, M.D., (*The Mind and the Brain*) demonstrates in his treatment of conditions like obsessive compulsive disorder that the brain is neuroplastic. Dr. Schwartz states that the mind can change the brain through neuroplasticity, which is the ability of neurons to rewire the brain.

The brain does change on its own developmentally and as a result of disease or injury but it is critical to understand that we have the power to use our mind to rearrange brain circuits through *focused attention and directed mental effort*.

The ability of the mind to change the brain is not a "theory". Using brain scans (F-MRI, PET, etc.) as proof we can see brain neurons in the process of functioning and changing. A dedicated program focused on our desires and goals will reorganize substructures of the brain.

In short, using focused attention and directed mental effort we can change brain circuitry. We have the ability to make significant inroads to problems like inappropriate anger responses, mood disorders and habitual thought processes. Within limits we are able to redesign the foundational properties of our physical and mental life in any way we choose.

## CHANGING YOUR REACTION TO ANGER

Passive thoughts are of limited value for changing neuroplasticity. "Why is Jerry talking like that to me? He shouldn't," versus, "The next time Jerry speaks angrily I will immediately walk away." Or, "When he yells at me I will leave the house and when I come back and he is calm, I will tell him marriage counseling is a necessity and if he isn't going I'm going by myself." Now you are talking to your mind definitively; you are training your brain to jump into a problem solving mode and think.

Wishy-washy self-talk in the face of anger is like whining, it gets you nowhere except further into your own mental muddle. Whereas directed mental activity clearly and systematically changes brain function.

To alter the negative flow of communication when anger and/or verbal abuse are directed at you, take charge. Whimpering and complaining, repeating old worn out talk that does not work, is out. Action is required.

Chapter Four describes the action-oriented steps needed when verbal abuse is a feature of your relationship. Once a day or once a month verbal abuse cannot be tolerated.

## CHAPTER FOUR

# I'M JUST NOT HAPPY...I LIVE WITH VERBAL ABUSE

**THE ABUSIVE MARRIAGE: IMMEDIATE FIVE-MINUTE SOLUTION**

Peace at any cost was Emily's motto. Emily learned in her first months of marriage to avoid her husband Jerry's nasty words and to keep peace. After a tongue lashing from Jerry, Emily's defeated, tearful apology mollified Jerry, but exacerbated Emily's unhappiness and did not solve their ongoing problems. Emily wanted Jerry to change, needed Jerry to change and felt he should change.

Changing herself hadn't occurred to Emily because she knew she was right and Jerry was wrong. So the habit, Jerry's verbal abuse followed by Emily's apology, continued for seven years.

Suddenly Emily decided seven years was long enough. She was sick and tired of peace at all costs and made a counseling appointment. In therapy Emily focused on altering her thoughts and reactions and gave up the idea that Jerry change. Emily learned and adopted the One-Minute Rule and the Five-Minute Solution. Her mental fog cleared; she became definitive and the marriage took a remarkable turn.

**EMILY: CHARGING OUT OF VERBAL ABUSE WITH A PLAN**

It was Emily's first session and she looked tense in spite of a half-smile on her face. Thirty-four years old, tall and trim, with floating white/blonde hair and green eyes, she sat stiffly on the edge of the couch facing me. Anxiety oozed from her voice, the strain evident in her face and eyes. In a rush Emily blurted out, "I've had a problem for seven years and I feel desperate.

"My husband, Jerry, acts like a woman who has monthly periods. He is mean and nasty for several days, and then he's nice for a week or two and then he's back to being a lunatic. I mean he has nice moods where he talks to me like I'm a person, well, actually like he should all the time, and then slowly day after day he begins to put me down. He sneers at me and is snide. That part doesn't bother me I'm so used to it. But when he starts screaming, I cannot not pay attention."

Now Emily is looking right at me, "I'm so pathetic. I hate to even tell you I put up with a man who acts like that. I know I can't change him but I keep trying to change myself so he'll stop treating me like he hates me. What's funny is that when he's in his nice mood he says he loves me. Does that make sense?

"It's like nice talk fools me into thinking that he actually loves me. Can a person scream at you and look like he hates you, practically foam at the mouth, and stand about two inches from your face yelling about how stupid you are and then love you, too?

"I think constantly about my life, about what to do. Should I leave? Should I stay? I tell him I won't put up with his behavior but then I do.

"My family can barely be around him. They've told me he is so disrespectful to me in his tone, look and words that he's lucky no one's punched him. I mean, what is wrong with me?

"I stopped working three years ago because Jerry urged me to. Jerry has his own business so we don't need money. My life was hectic when I worked because I had no time to take care of the house, pay attention to my family, or handle all the other errands and details of life.

But, the problem with not working is think-time. I think, think, think.

"My thinking about the situation is constant, like 'things will change if I am nicer or more loving or ignore him or tell him to knock it off,' but my thinking gets me nowhere because it's hard to actually do what I think. The situations never seem appropriate. I had this same problem in my first marriage except that my first husband would hit me and be nasty. I didn't leave him until I was in some state that was like a nervous breakdown. I don't want to get to that point again."

Emily paused and then said, "I want you to tell me what to do. You probably won't, though."

I said, "You are right. I won't tell you what to do. What we will do is talk about your thoughts, feelings and life events to discover what keeps you rooted in worry thinking and fear. In the meantime," I told Emily, "here is a method to immediately alter your mind set and keep you from stepping into your husband's angry vortex."

## ONE-MINUTE RULE

To consciously take control of yourself this is what you do: Think again! When you feel caught in circular, upsetting, negative thinking immediately use the One-Minute Rule. The second you hear that inner worry, dialogue stop and take charge of your mind for one minute.

Try it right now. For one minute concentrate and repeat a simple phrase like, "I feel calm." Notice how the mind wants to wander?

This is important. If your heart is racing because of Jerry's words and behavior, order yourself to feel calm with slow breathing. You will be able to repeat "I feel calm" approximately 40 times. Keep concentrating while you talk to yourself; don't let your mind ramble around or dart into other thoughts.

If Jerry's behavior distracts you from the One Minute Rule, start again. It is better for you to be focusing in on inner calm than focusing out on agitated anger or rage.

With tenacious daily use the One-Minute Rule works to establish a new pathway in your brain just like consistent arm exercises build your bicep. For example, when used consistently with feelings of anxiety the Rule reduces anxiety. When you are concentrating on "I feel calm" you are not thinking other thoughts, which means that moment is free of anxiety and at the same time you learn that anxiety does not have control. You are in control.

The One-Minute Rule is important for control and also because what you think is what you are. William James, a famous twentieth century psychologist, once said, "You are what you think all day long." Thinking produces feelings.

Thoughts and feelings are like a magnet that attract or detract understanding to you or to others. Emily's distress and subconscious anger are detrimental for her and undoubtedly picked up by her husband through expression and tone so she may feel she has been conciliatory toward her husband. Still, unless he is stupid, he understands she is upset.

Exactly what is Emily thinking about her husband? I asked her to imagine repeating her inner dialogue out loud and guess: Are those words about Jerry problem-solving? Do you feel better? Emily said, "No. I'm mad and sad at the same time."

Once the One-Minute Rule is in place, deliberately set a time to think for five minutes. For example, decide that in the car you will use five minutes as think time. Check the time and give yourself time for the Five-Minute Solution and actually tell yourself, "First, what do I want and, second, what action can I take." Think specifically about what you want and decide what action, thought or behavior will move you in your desired direction.

This is practice thinking. You are not going to act on desires or actions at this moment in time. You are raising possibilities with yourself. The point of the Five-Minute Solution is to settle down, be serious about yourself and your situation and think about problem solving instead of filling your mind with distress.

## EMILY'S ISSUES

Emily has married the same personality twice, an individual who cannot respect or listen to another person, whose mouth is out of control. If she leaves husband number two without methods to consciously take charge of herself and understand what drives her to accept abusive talk and emotional tyranny, we can guess that her next intimate relationship will repeat the first two. Emily's attitudes, feelings, behavior, and life experiences are an expression of low self-esteem that she keeps alive and well through thought repetition.

Emily has refused to take herself seriously by pretending that by twisting herself into what she imagined Jerry wanted she could change him. Using this logic Emily is turning her life over to her husband by tiptoeing around him, putting up with disrespect, fearing his outbursts and allowing Her Majesty, the baby inside her, to cry, whine and cower in fear. "Oh, no, what if he yells at me or says nasty things to me? That is awful. I can't stand it when he is mean to me. He shouldn't talk to me like that or look at me like that or behave that way." Well, Guess what? Jerry will continue to be himself.

Regardless of the specific details of the story or the struggle, whether the relationship is distant, mean spirited, nasty, or just plain dull and boring, the form is the same. Constant thinking about the relationship does not mean change. It simply means that Emily is grinding the relationship down with obsessive thoughts, continuously reiterating to herself that Jerry is mean-spirited and allowing those habitual thoughts to color daily life with fear. In other words, Emily is a part of the ongoing drama of abuse.

Emily is very good at conscious thinking; she pays attention to her inner dialogue. However, without a plan of action Emily's habit-driven, inner Jerry-diatribe simply piles more angst on years of emotional muck.

**IMMEDIATE PROBLEM:** Emily fears Jerry's words. She acts as though she has no backbone. She lacks conviction, acts frozen, and cannot seem to act on either intellect or intuition.

**IMMEDIATE SOLUTION:** Verbal and physical action: When Jerry began his threats and intimidation techniques in the past Emily felt anxious and fearful. Now, to settle herself down and eliminate fear, Emily is to first think about his loud voice and offensive words as the voice of a baby crying at the top of its lungs, very annoying but harmless. Second, Emily is to avoid looking directly at Jerry's menacing face and scary grimaces. (70% of communication lies in facial nuances and body behavior.) Third, she is to continually respond calmly with any of the following (or for as long as she can stand it), knowing her words are meant to sooth herself, not Jerry, during his tirade.

1. "Yes, I understand that's how you feel."
2. "Yes. I can be unpleasant-distant-nasty-foolish-charming-wonderful-thoughtful at times."
3. "Spit it all out. Go on. Tell me more."
4. "It must be terrible to be so upset."

It made Emily laugh to think about talking to Jerry as though she were his psychologist and she felt better having a plan that put her in control of herself.

Mental Action: Emily dedicates herself to conscious, solution-oriented thoughts and when old fear-generating habits sneak into her mind she tells herself:

1. Stop it!
2. For one minute repeat calming words, using the One-Minute Rule.
3. Then ask yourself, "What action can I take right now?"
4. Proceed with physical action, i.e., jumping jacks, push-ups and mental action, the Five-Minute Solution.
5. Solve this moment, the next hour and the rest of the day. Set up a plan for today. You will not allow your mind to roll into tomorrow, next week, next year or last year.
6. You will seize this day, develop this day, and enjoy this day in any way possible.

At first Emily reported that her thoughts reverted to what Jerry should do and how upset she was by his words. Slowly but surely, like a drumbeat, Emily inundated her mind with the need to focus on clarity of action this moment. She had to keep pulling her thoughts back to calm control and focus on desire.

**LONG TERM SOLUTION:** Take charge of yourself. Learn to speak your mind, first through inner dialogue and second, through verbalizing calm, appropriate, heartfelt words. Find peace within yourself:

1. Through therapy gain an understanding of why you need to have your husband hammer yourself-esteem while you give in and give up.
2. Shift focus from distress to goal.
3. No more questions about "Why" Jerry acts as he does. Jerry will not change. Cement in your mind that Jerry's words and behavior are written in stone. Figure out your "why".

4. Plan a future with Jerry or without him. If your future is with Jerry, learn how to accept his behavior.

Six months into therapy Emily decided to divorce Jerry. Jerry, much to Emily's surprise, screamed, cried and told Emily, "I cannot live without you. I love you. Please, I'm begging, don't leave me." Emily was shocked by his protestations of love but did not drop the divorce. Instead, she asked her attorney to put the divorce on hold to determine if there was any depth to Jerry's words.

Was Jerry reacting with love words to stay in control or was there actually hope for the marriage? Emily needed time. As much as Jerry tried to manage himself, his old behavior kept inserting itself into the relationship. Emily wavered back and forth but eventually decided to divorce.

Through therapy and conscious attention to thoughts and feelings Emily discovered that she no longer cared whether Jerry "really" loved her or not. Fortunately Emily's mind had not turned to mush the brain-torture-mush that occurs when self-esteem trampling is delivered on a daily basis and the recipient is incapable of warding off the blows.

## CHAPTER FIVE

# I'M JUST NOT HAPPY...I KNOW MY SITUATION IS ABUSIVE BUT I SEEM INCAPABLE OF LEAVING

## HABITUAL THOUGHTS

Just like Emily we all tend to flounder in unhappiness rather than focus on possible solutions because we regard thoughts that come to mind as the truth.

Thoughts that come to mind when problems occur are mental habits that pop up from a storehouse of automatic responses that evolved in our relationship life. Most of us do not recognize the mental habits that run our life and instead of looking inside and taking responsibility for our unhappiness, we whine about our partner's behavior, loudly or subtly, as though we are helpless.

Relationships should be easy, a snap, requiring little except our presence, we think. Even though we have had bad relationships and seen disastrous marriages between parents or aunts, uncles, brothers and sisters we are surprised by our own unhappiness.

"But," you say, "Why change? I have these thoughts with good reason. My partner is acting in ways that are intolerable." I say that's part of your problem, clinging to habitual thoughts rather than accepting that he will act as he has always acted. If you want a marital problem solved, you bring your consciousness to bear, figure out a solution, pursue or modify it until it sticks and if it doesn't work try something else. And assume that your husband or wife will not change.

If I told you I have a beige couch but it should be purple and I'm mad that it's beige, you would think I was crazy. You'd say, "Get over it or buy a new couch!" Getting mad at your husband's habitual behavior is bad behavior on your part. Those negative thoughts keep you and your marriage mired in distress.

Solving habitual thought patterns requires consciousness, today, not occasional consciousness, but total consciousness this moment. Unhappiness is mired in negative quicksand muck that sticks like glue. To pull yourself out, ratchet up your positive emotions and focus one moment at a time on a positive phrase, something you admire about your partner, and then repeat the phrase to yourself for one minute on and off throughout the day.

Then you might say to me, "Why would I focus on admiring my spouse when I have a problem with him?" At this particular moment in time the overall issues may not be solved but you can stop hopelessly circling around your disturbance with him. You married him, he must have some redeeming qualities so while you begin the relationship solution process, you calm and soothe yourself with positive thoughts.

## ABUSING THE SELF

We have random thoughts and we also have random feelings. There are people who are *Thoughters* and people who are *Feelers*. A Thoughter is without judgment, an airhead. Thoughters are just that; they live by any thought that comes to mind and ignore feelings. Their rationale is, "Because a thought came to mind it must have meaning." No. We have 60,000 thoughts a day and they do not all have meaning.

A Feeler reacts solely to feelings. He or she is a very emotional person who is swayed by any feeling thought. Thinking past the immediate feeling does not happen. Susan is a Feeler whose judgment is also impaired because her intellect cannot dislodge emotions that cloud her mind.

## MONSTER ABUSE

### SUSAN: THE FEELER

Susan is beside herself. She is not happy. She has lived 16 years with her husband, Steve, an occasionally physically abusive, always emotionally abusive husband. The final insult, Susan says, is that after all she has put up with Steve is having an affair with his associate and flaunting it.

Susan lives in fear like every abused person. In spite of Steve's vicious words and the affair she cannot bring herself to tell him goodbye. Susan says, "The minute I assert myself he backs down. He's sorry. He loves me. Then, believe it or not, I feel good.

"I can't constantly be mad at him, it upsets me too much. Steve ridicules me and denies what he has just said and then he speaks nicely and I melt. I'm a fool and I know it." Susan grins. Her grin denies that she feels a fool.

The criteria for Susan's life are her feelings. Either she is filled with anguish, feeling tormented by his abuses or giddy with Steve's "love" for her.

Susan is living a lie. Looking in from the outside her life appears perfect. Susan, 46, has a administrative position with a large corporation. Her husband, Steve, 51, is tall, handsome and well spoken with a career in a prestigious business. They own a home on a lake with boats, cars and even a plane.

Susan thinks others view her as a confident professional with a good marriage. People are not stupid. They hear his tone and the way he puts her down. Steve speaks to Susan as if she is a demented servant and

Susan allows Steve to talk down to her, chastise, deride and scold her. Her rationale: "I don't have it in me to keep arguing."

Nevertheless, Susan bravely took two steps, revealing her real life in therapy and opening up to friends. Talking about her situation was the first step but Susan cannot take the next action-oriented step to separate, instead, she is drawn back to her emotionally chaotic life and soon leaves counseling.

Six months later, drowning in fear, Susan returns to therapy. Susan now knows more than she ever wanted to know about her husband. Secretly accessing Steve's computer, Susan discovered pornographic material that could ruin his career. Steve is involved in pornographic chat rooms where people flaunt naked body parts, including his own, and discuss deviant sexual activities. He is also emailing a variety of women while continuing an extra-marital affair. Steve is a busy guy with no boundaries.

Susan plans to leave, she wants to leave, she is in a dither trying to gather things together to leave the house and, yet, she never quite makes it out the door. Because her feelings are paramount she has no resolve. She sways like a leaf in the wind. Susan is lost; herself, her identity, is a reflector and reactor to Steve.

A new wrinkle. Steve claims he has cancer. He needs Susan. He is scared. She is the caretaker and must care for him.

Therapeutically working to steady Susan's feelings while she grasps the significance of her husband's behavior, in other words, step outside her ego to gain insight, is slow going and ultimately impossible. Her need to remain bonded with her oppressor is profound, for while Susan's intellect seeks help in therapy, her emotions overwhelm any possibility of action.

Three years later Susan and Steve are still together and Susan continues to tell her story saying, "I plan to leave," but at this point no one is listening.

## FEELINGS ARE PRECEEDED BY THOUGHTS

We live life in our minds where perception and interpretation fuel feeling and expression. Thoughts are reality just as a lamp or a car is real. What you do is dependent upon what you think; thoughts move you to action.

Your feelings are preceded by neutral thoughts, thoughts that excite, or thoughts that depress emotional areas in your brain. Occasionally, however, you experience primitive, reactive feelings. For example, a person driving the car in front of you slams on the brakes, which results in a startle, fight or flight reflex. But, other than fight or flight, major illness or accident, the life you lead has to do with the spin you put on your thoughts.

Since you cannot see the whirring of your brain, you simply experience the outcome. You do not have a Plexiglas head where you can see brain functions light up. There isn't a click or a snap or a bright light in your eyes that lets you know: Warning! Danger! Change thoughts!

With unhappiness we develop habit-driven thoughts and behavior to manage distress. We attempt to bring rational thought and behavior to mind to twist unhappiness around so that life can run smoothly but then, just like addicts, we repeat old, automatic thoughts to ourselves, the same words to our spouse and behavior that has never worked, over and over and over.

When the snap of a marital disconnection occurs old whiney thoughts comfortably fall into place: "I just want to be happy." (The implication here is that your spouse is responsible and blankets you with syrup of unhappiness.) "Why does he bring up the past?" "He knows when he does that and says that, I am hurt." (The implication is that your spouse is a magical thinker who deliberately sets out to hurt you.) Because dialogue automatically comes to mind or feelings occur, neither thoughts nor emotions must be entertained or accepted as fact.

Unless you actively, consciously pay attention to the habitual configurations you have fed into your brain over the years, you return to the trough of negative feelings, just like a drug addict returns to a drug of choice again and again.

## JUNE IS JUST NOT HAPPY WITH HER HUSBAND'S FLIRTATIOUS BEHAVIOR

The essence and theme of June's problem: Historical words stored in the mind without a solution remain active, like an ongoing infection, tearing and ripping at the relationship. June has been unhappy with disrespectful and, in her eyes, abusive behavior for years and feels she will not continue to participate, but she is stymied and thinks divorce may be the only answer.

However long your marriage, if you are experiencing unhappiness now, this is the time to take charge of yourself. It is not a good idea to entertain upsetting thought patterns and feelings for 40 years as June did.

## JUNE AND HAL: HABITUAL THOUGHTS AND FEELINGS

Although I had difficulty understanding June's entire message on my voice mail I did understand her desperation. "Please, please help me", she said. Since she indicated that she lived at least an hour and a half away from my office, I called her back intent on giving her both a referral and a crisis center number to call immediately. When I reached June she insisted that she must see me, only me, as her trusted friend had referred her.

We set up an appointment early the next day.

Given her frantic message I'm not sure what I expected that morning, but I was surprised. June is 75, Korean, dignified and elegant. Her skin is clear and unwrinkled. She dresses stylishly and from the back appears to be a young woman.

June is unhappy as a result of ongoing issues in her marriage. She told me that her husband, Hal, 72, who retired three years ago, has not respected her from "day one," that fateful day they met in Korea.

June owned the tailoring shop on the American Air Force Base in Korea and when Hal came in to pick up shirts, it was love at first sight. Hal left Korea a year later and vowed he would be back to marry June. Hal kept his word.

When June and Hal went to the base commander for authorization to marry, necessary in the military overseas, June reports that instead of the hassle others had experienced the Commander said to Hal, "Where did you find this lovely woman?"

We begin to understand the powerful affect respect and admiration have on June when the commander's words reverberate through time and continue to give her pleasure.

Hal's behavior at home has been the cement in their relationship. June told me, "At home Hal tells me he loves me and is very nice to me, but if we are out he acts like I am not around. The last straw was our grandson's wedding on Saturday. He ignored me and stared at other women, making eye contact and then talking flirtatiously, still—at his age!

"When we eat out he spends his time ogling other women. He is blatant and I find it disgusting. When I talk to him about his behavior or anything else that bothers me he says, 'You don't understand' or 'You don't get it.' That's his way to shut me up."

While she told her story June began to cry, then quickly apologized for her tears. I told June that my office would not know what to do without emotions. I asked

June if her husband embarrasses her. "Yes," she whispered with tiny tears spilling from her eyes. "Yes, yes."

**IMMEDIATE PROBLEM:** June's habitual thoughts and feelings as she reacts to Hal's social behavior. Feelings are messages. Deciphering the message is the difficulty.

**IMMEDIATE SOLUTION:** Drop habitual thoughts, words and behavior that expect Hal to be different. June is to take charge of her restaurant behavior—not Hal's. June's messages to her husband have never worked, never made a difference. Why would saying them again effect change?

The next time plans are made to dine out June will inform Hal nicely but firmly that she likes being with him and would like to eat out but she is uncomfortable when he stares and talks to other women and finds this behavior unacceptable.

If Hal says that he does not look longingly at other women or states that June is imagining things, June replies that she is aware that that is how he thinks. However, that is not how she thinks or feels and she indicates further that either their dinner plans are off or that she will decide at the restaurant whether his behavior is tolerable.

And June will be prepared. She will drive her own car or if she is uncomfortable driving alone and the behavior persists, she will get a taxi. If she is unable to follow through she is letting Hal know that she has no backbone and is all talk.

**LONG TERM SOLUTION:** Live in this moment. If June is feeling distressed, think! "Why am I distressed?" These feelings are real. Emotions are to be examined with her intellect and taken seriously. Are these feelings habit driven and historical? What are the feelings about and what can she do about them?

June is to take charge of her feelings and thoughts, eliminating habitual dialogue with herself and the same old discussion with her husband that gets her nowhere but upset and angry. June is to use the One-Minute Rule to calm and alter thoughts. Then decide on a plan for herself, for her words and behavior.

## THOUGHTS DIRECT BEHAVIOR

Hal's refusal to acknowledge his behavior has stymied June. June fails to recognize that when Hal does not respond to what she is saying, and, in fact, denies her reality, her words are meaningless. Rather than continuously react to Hal, June is to be the actor.

Action carries a risk, however. It is important to assess what is the worst that can happen: Hal will not like the talk; he will get angry; he will refuse to go out to eat; or he will change his behavior. It is very important for June to recognize potential consequences and decide whether she is up to each of these possibilities before she talks to Hal.

June shocked me. Immediately after our first therapy session June told me that she took charge of herself and quit "acting like a baby." June said it was a miracle. Hal did not know what to make of the difference in June but he did respond positively. His disrespectful restaurant behavior collapsed. One success does not mean back to business as usual, rather, June needs to be vigilant and continue her staunch attitude. She will not put up with disrespectful behavior.

June's experience in therapy is an example of thought alteration that has the potential to transform a marriage so completely, so radically and so marvelously that after a few short months a different, positive marriage experience emerges.

## TRAIN YOUR BRAIN

Conscious desire to solve problems is the starting point of all positive change. Studies of the brain show that the mind is malleable and can be consciously reprogrammed.

If we were able to watch our brain in action we would see that the brain sparkles and flashes as brain neurons are changed. Even when you are 90, any thought, behavior or feeling habit that you want to change can be changed.

In other words, ground-in mental habits, which imply helplessness, are not in your brain to stay unless you lay down, play dead and allow your mind to continue rambling through historical thought patterns. How you respond when you are unhappy is up to you. You have the power to train your brain.

Chapter Five elucidates the experience of affair crisis that shocks the system and produces the experience of emotional helplessness. A survival and revival plan is restorative.

## CHAPTER SIX

# I'M JUST NOT HAPPY...I SUSPECT MY PARTNER IS HAVING AN AFFAIR

### KAREN'S POSITION: AN AFFAIR? YOU DON'T UNDERSTAND. I AM INNOCENT.

Karen is frantic. Crying on the phone, her husband does not understand the relationship between her and a friend. Can she come in and talk about it?

Karen, 36, has the look of an all-American girl. Her blonde hair is pulled back in a thick braid and she has very little make-up over her freckles. She works part-time at a "small job." Her husband, Jeff, 38, is a computer programmer.

Sitting anxiously on the edge of the couch in my office Karen begins her first session by pleading her case, begging for understanding—and possibly forgiveness. Eyes red and Kleenex at the ready, Karen begins.

"I am unhappy. No, I am miserable. I have an old friend, Bobby, who I talk to on the phone. I give him advice; I'm his shoulder to cry on. That is all.

"I just discovered that my husband, Jeff, has been taping my calls and believes that I am having an affair. Nothing could be further from the truth. I love Jeff, I tell him that all the time. I have absolutely no feelings for Bobby."

Between wiping her eyes and blowing her nose Karen continued, "What's more, Jeff has informed friends, family, and I guess anyone he talks to that I am having an affair. He even took our 15-year-old, Rachel, with him to spy on Bobby. I am so mad and so embarrassed and humiliated.

"Jeff asked me to stop calling Bobby and I said 'No.' I am not doing anything wrong and you can't control me. My first husband was a control freak, among other things, and I won't put up with someone trying to order me around." Karen looked at me for several seconds, and then said; "I'm thinking Jeff wants a divorce so I'm starting to look for a full time job. I need to be prepared."

I asked Karen, "Do you want a divorce?"

Puffing herself up Karen said, "No, absolutely not. I love my husband and I want the marriage but I will not be told what to do. I said to Jeff, 'We need marriage counseling'. He said he would come but I thought I better tell you about the situation first."

Karen wants to make sure I understand her feelings before I hear the other side of the story. I asked Karen to have Jeff call me; I'd like to meet with him before the three of us begin marriage counseling.

**KAREN'S THOUGHTS:** What is Karen's inner dialogue? Karen thinks: "I have a right to talk to a friend." "Jeff can't tell me what to do." "How dare he intrude on my privacy?" "Jeff knows I love him. He's deliberately turning my phone calls against me. We were happy until he started this trouble."

These defensive thoughts do not solve Karen's problem, but they do incense her and put her in a combative relationship position.

**JEFF'S POSITION: "I HAVE BEEN BETRAYED."** Jeff appeared promptly for his first appointment. Jeff is about 5'7", small-boned with thinning blonde hair. He waited for me to begin. I told him I had talked to Karen and since people in marriages often have different points of views about situations, I would like to hear his.

Jeff had obviously thought about what he was going to tell me. "This crisis began with a phone bill. I looked at Karen's list of phone calls and my heart stopped. I was shocked. She had 40 calls to one number. 40 calls! Can you imagine? And it was a number I was unfamiliar with.

"Karen is an outgoing person, a chatter box, and has lots of people calling her and vice versa. She's always telling me about her sister or a friend's problems but I hadn't heard of anyone having a major problem worth 40 calls.

"Of course, I dialed the number, got an answering device, and I wasn't sure who it was but for sure it was a male voice. From then on I became a detective. I looked at old telephone bills and there it was, call after call after call.

"I'm sorry that I did some of the things I did like confiding in my daughter and talking to everyone in the world. I feel stupid now. I should have kept it to myself.

"Instead I proceeded to tape Karen's calls and what I heard just made me sick. She and this guy talked sexually—explicit sex talk. I have to say Karen is more sexual than I am; she always initiates sex. Because she's so sexual what she was saying freaked me out.

"I'm still crazed. This guy she says is an old friend I met once, but I also know she slept with him before we were married.

"Karen claims she does not care about him, he's just a friend, but she refuses to stop talking to him so to me that means she has feelings for him. Why did she keep it a secret if it didn't amount to anything?

"I can't make sense out of it. In a marriage, who talks secretly to another person 40 times in one month unless an affair is going on? She says it's not an affair. I say what else do you call it?"

**JEFF'S THOUGHTS:** "I have to get a divorce. I can't live with someone who is involved with someone else. How could she talk sexually to someone else? What else has she been doing?" Jeff's obsession with Karen's "affair" keeps him agitated and emotionally traumatized circling the same information without relief.

What is in Karen's mind? She says she is absolutely not having an affair. Jeff says if it is not an affair, what is it? Jeff feels that the emotional carnage will color the marriage forever.

The word affair is a bomb bursting in air, damage spewing everywhere. Even if Karen had half an affair, a telephone affair, like a child she kept it a secret because she knew talking to another man would cause difficulty in her marriage.

Karen's behavior fits the word affair. Affair means an illicit secret relationship. No wiggling out of it. And Karen's refusal to stop calling Bobby is not smart. She is going to be true to her right to be independent while she is living in a dependent relationship and loyal to her telephone buddy but not to her husband.

If the shoe were on the other foot Karen would jump up and down, scream and yell, and be hurt to the quick. She obviously found a way to talk herself into the idea that regardless of content she was talking to a friend and, consequently, anything goes. Karen said this is how she talks to her female friends. Possibly.

## DISCOVERING WHAT IS REAL

## CAN FRIGHTENED THOUGHT PATTERNS BE ALTERED? SEVERAL SCENARIOS

1. Jeff has an ongoing experience of distress justified by external reality. His bitterness bubbles and boils as his inner dialogue seethes with fear and resentment toward Karen. Can Jeff redirect his thought processes?
2. Jeff states that he loves Karen and wants the marriage. Karen states that she loves Jeff and

wants the marriage. Do their thoughts corroborate their words? Are these words real or a momentary fear of loss?
3. Can Jeff calm his brain through this troubled period?
4. Karen has deliberately set herself up for trouble and negative attention. What was her motivation? Is this a telephone repair affair which is meant to get Jeff's attention (*In Affairs: Emergency Tactics* by Carol Rhodes a repair affair is meant to get a partner's attention and change the relationship) or a means to leave the relationship?

**IMMEDIATE SOLUTION: CALM YOUR MIND. DECIDE WHAT YOU WANT: MARRIAGE? IF SO:**

**KAREN**

1. Bring the emotional escalator to a halt by attention to negatively charged thoughts. Replace them with a mantra of calm and patience, force patience since impulsivity is your forte.
2. A powerful technique for instant change is physical action. Walk around the house, walk or run outside, do pushups, lift weights. Immediately catch and stop each thought about Bobby with action.
3. Use the One-Minute Rule.
4. Put negative thoughts on paper, then tear them up and throw the paper and the thought away. Negative thoughts are to be discussed with your therapist only, not with yourself or friends.

**JEFF**

1. Obsessing about Karen's phone calls are stopped now.

2. When you hear your mind whipping up anguish and anger, tell yourself, "Stop it!"
3. Continuously focus on your desire: a happy marriage. Whether or not you can trust Karen only time will reveal.

Karen's response to an immediate solution, "I know Jeff will bring up Bobby and then what should I do?" Acknowledge that Jeff's thoughts and feelings are difficult for him. Do not respond defensively. You are a grown woman in control of thoughts, words and behavior. Take control of yourself and focus on the fact that your husband is in distress.

Jeff basically said the same thing. "I can't pretend everything is o.k. I can't spend a day with Karen and ignore what she has done." Well, then, I guess a solution is hopeless. You are a leaf in the wind without control. When you are at work do you say every word that comes to mind?

To both Karen and Bobby: Quit mental dialoguing as though you have been programmed by this situation and cannot manage yourself. If you want your marriage to change, you change. There isn't any magic and you know it. You take control of yourself one-minute, one hour and one day at a time.

## LONG TERM SOLUTION: TRAIN THE BRAIN

The possibility of an affair damages trust, which is the foundation of a committed relationship, and may crack trust for all time. To re-establish trust Karen cuts Bobby and his phone calls out of her life and when her mind wanders into her lame defense, which is, "I will not be controlled," knock it off. You cannot have it both ways. Either you are married and committed or you are free to have phone liaisons with the opposite sex.

First Karen walks a straight marital path and stops rationalizing. Second, and this is crucial, she uncovers the need for attention, multiple men or an inability to be faithful.

Jeff lifts a corner of his trauma and focuses on the idea that Karen is unusual, that he has always trusted her and known that she will say and do anything and that these calls do not constitute an affair. Then, and this is crucial, Jeff does not allow his mind to retort, "Yes, but..."

It is easy to see that Jeff and Karen's thoughts are their life. In crisis we are primitive as we repeat dramatic words to ourselves over and over trying to find our way out of trauma. The emotional thought escalator is in motion: up and down, up and down.

## DAY ALONE

Try a Day Alone with one another. Plan a Day Alone without children, phones or responsibilities. On the Day Alone you are not allowed one negative word. Marital history is not discussed. Whatever thought comes to mind; if the thought is negative it is not allowed out of your mouth.

Think of the Day Alone as peak performance in your marriage, searching for flow. You will act toward your spouse in exactly those ways that you want from him or her—without expectations that this should be what your spouse is giving to you.

A day alone with a positive, loving focus is a breather, an opportunity to look and think about yourself and your partner. At the end of the day when you are walking back into your responsible life again, plan daily words and behaviors to stay on a loving track.

## POSITIVE THOUGHTS

Thoughts determine happiness or unhappiness this moment, this hour and this day. You can do anything you desire with your mind. Keep reminding yourself that you are in charge of your mind and when thoughts come to mind take a look at those thoughts. Do you want to continue misery? Do stressful thoughts and words get you anywhere? ATTENTION TO DESIRE, LOVE AND A HAPPY MARRIAGE, WILL BRING RESULTS just as attention to anger and hurt feelings will bring results—but not the results you say you desire.

Working through their issues was difficult and at times felt hopeless but Karen and Jeff stuck with it and are together one year after marriage counseling ended and report that they are "doing well."

Heather, on the other hand, is not doing well. She recently discovered a secret that put her long-term marriage in jeopardy. The tip off began with Bob's emotional disappearing act.

## BOB'S SECRET

What happened to Bob? After years of marriage Bob would not respond to Heather for days on end. Bob had always been the strong, silent type but now when Heather tried to chat with Bob or ask him questions, Bob simply stared, sometimes nodded his head and turned away and that drove Heather crazy. Heather began with her usual screaming, yelling and out-of-control anger. When that didn't work she threatened divorce, threatened to tell everyone about his behavior, threatened to turn their grown children against him but in the end Bob took charge. He moved out.

In desperation Heather called for therapy for herself.

## MARRIAGE OVERVIEW

Heather reports that her 25-year marriage to Bob has always been stable and solid until Bob's distancing act began. Bob is quiet and steady, while Heather is the emotional conduit, volatile and argumentative.

Heather's grown kids think that she is overbearing, bossy, and often angry but, according to Heather, Bob would not take charge, never had, so she was the villain as she filled the vacuum with her own mother's combative style, "Someone had to manage and control the kids and run the household."

## HISTORY

Action-oriented, able to manage many tasks, Heather's anger had fueled her energy as she mothered four children through ballet, soccer, basketball, tennis, acrobatic, piano lessons, and up into college while at the same time she was working her own way through college. Finally, the kids were launched.

Heather now is a tenured teacher and she and Bob have just finished building a beautiful home on a lake. During the year the house was being built Bob was never around and if he was he did not interact. Unless Heather asked a concrete, direct question, silence was his mode. Their emotional connection ceased to exist. Even Heather's anger failed to arouse Bob. He just looked, and walked away.

Heather came to therapy because she said she was "going crazy." She thought her husband was depressed, having some kind of mid life crisis or having a nervous breakdown.

Afro-American solidly built with words to match, 53 year-old Heather cried on and off while she described her life with Bob. Heather said, "I'm scared. Bob has gone into a shell and I'm afraid he is going to lose his job. He's a CPA and, in addition, he supervises a large office, maybe 50 people. He has to be able to talk and make decisions.

"But, mainly, I can't stand the silent treatment. Bob's never been talkative, but he would respond and we could chat. Now, nothing. He won't even answer questions about the new house. You know when you're building a house there are a million details that have to be decided. He's totally blank. Not only that, he's always been a handy man, taking care of tasks around the house. Now, nothing."

Blowing her nose, talking through her sobs, Heather continued, "I'm sick of it! I've been screaming at him. He just looks at me and walks away. I've always gotten mad and yelled but this is ridiculous. I'm way over the edge with my anger.

"In my defense I have to get his attention and this seemed to be the only way until he refused to look at me or to respond. I asked him if he wants to be married. He says he doesn't know. What kind of an answer is that? I'm at my wit's end. I can't stand it."

Emotionally driven people experience their feelings accelerating when they're frustrated and, if that is their only tactic it works to a point. Others tiptoe around and stay vigilant to make sure they are not the displeasure trigger. At the same time the family learns that it is not fun to be the butt end of a person's anger.

Heather both saw herself as the villain and as the wounded, trapped person. Anger was her management tool and throughout her marriage she had given anger free rein. In the meantime, Bob has chosen to react unemotionally to distance himself.

Talking quietly to Heather to get her attention, I said, "Let's start by calming down. "Heather continued her high pitched, emotional focus, "What about Bob?"

Can she control Bob? No. Does she want to? Of course. Managing another person's behavior, emotion, or thoughts is rationally foolish and, yet, Heather was in the business of demanding that her husband act in a proscribed fashion that fits her comfort zone. Over the long haul this imbalance evidently reached an end point for Bob.

## THE SLEUTH

Heather became Sherlock Holmes and found the reason for Bob's withdrawal. Withdrawal's name was Joanne.

Joanne and Bob had worked together for 10 years. Evidently their friendship turned into romance a few years ago and Bob, although never confessing any serious involvement, acknowledged his attraction.

Now Heather is furious. She cannot believe Bob is involved with a "piece of s---" like Joanne. Now she knows. Now she understands. Now what?

**IMMEDIATE SOLUTION**: Bob is living with his brother but he is more often home with Heather, speaking to her, in fact, carrying on conversations. For months Heather has been modifying her behavior, learning to control her anger, which has not been easy. Heather "allows" Bob to be silent, without recriminations. At this time, there is no intimacy, sex, or shared feelings, but there is peace and there are possibilities for the relationship, at least in Heather's mind.

**LONG TERM SOLUTION:** Heather learned to take charge of herself by taking charge of her emotions, shutting her mouth and changing thoughts. She looks at her watch, gives herself five minutes, and if necessary walks out of the room and does not respond regardless of the provocation of her own thoughts.

**THE PLAN: CONSCIOUS CONDITIONING**

To develop a muscle beyond what is the "norm" for you, you actively, regularly build that muscle and over time, watch it grow and expand. Since your brain is part of your body, it also needs exercise. However, even if you decide to exercise either your brain or your muscles you will naturally resist and deny what you had planned: You don't have time; you are too tired; you are going to be too bulky, as in weight lifting for women.

Someone wise once said, "What you resist, persists." In the resistant mode you ignore any encouraging or positive thought. When that happens, fragmented, oppositional thinking, automatic old, negative thoughts come to mind and you do not dispute or resist them. You succumb.

Combating or waging war on non-productive or destructive thoughts is simple and yet difficult because those old thoughts are real to you. You produced the thought. You are responsible for each thought. It is yours. Habitual thoughts return to your mind again and again and are experienced as real and true. Not a problem. You produced the thoughts, now you recognize the thoughts for what they are—old and unproductive.

Take action when oppositional, negative thoughts take over. Stop the thought. It is simple; it is easy. Say to yourself, "Stop it right now." Talk to yourself as though you are a child. Replace the automatic thought with a desired conscious thought. This is you training your brain.

## ALTER THOUGHTS

Although most of us choose to behave as if our brain is on its own and we have no control when we feel unhappy, we can alter thoughts in any way or at any time we choose.

However, we are habit-driven and not crazy about taking charge or blame for our life and often blame our spouse, "If he hadn't said that I would not have been upset." Or we pull out the incompetent card and beat ourselves up. "What was I thinking?" "I'm an idiot." "That was stupid." Guilt plays a big hand in avoiding responsibility, "God is punishing me," or "If I had fixed meat loaf for dinner like he wanted he wouldn't be upset." Nice try, instead of thinking, being real and taking charge, blame is a gloss-over; the pretend blame game does not work.

Blame yourself, blame your job or blame your husband but the end result is you are still stuck. Connie is an example. For years Connie was happy in her marriage and, then, suddenly she felt unhappy and blamed her husband.

## THE EMOTIONAL AFFAIR

In her first therapy session Connie, 37, said, "I'm here because I'm just not happy. Other people, my sister, would think I'm crazy because I have a nice house, a new car, a fur coat, and diamond earrings but I haven't been happy for a long time.

"This feeling began two years ago when my husband, Ryan, and I went on a vacation to Cancun which we've done since we've been married. We always take two vacations a year but something strange happened two years ago. I did not want to come back home and go to work. I know that doesn't sound unusual but I actually love working.

"I'll give you a little background about myself first. When my husband and I married 14 years ago we agreed that we would save our money and retire in our forties. We are both very responsible; we work and we save. We met in high school. As you can see I am overweight and I was even then a 'fatty'. In spite of feeling self-conscious I decided I wanted to marry Ryan and I seriously went after him.

"My pursuit worked. We dated five years, got married, decided not to have children, to buy a house as soon as we could and that's exactly what we did. This house is our third and it is beautiful. We had a plan and worked it.

"It seems like out of the blue I woke up two years ago and thought, 'All we do is work.' My husband works 28 or 29 days out of a month. That doesn't leave much time for us to be together and in the past that was all right. I was so crazy about him that whatever he said or did was just fine.

"On my days off, Saturday and Sunday, I would make lunches and drive to his plant just to be with him. I really did hand stands for him, anything he needed or wanted I took care of if I could. No more.

"Now I don't want to be home when he's off work. Ryan is affectionate only when we are having sex and that lasts 15 minutes max. I used to want more. Now I'm glad it only lasts 15 minutes.

"Listen to this. He says to me 'Do you want to be poked?' That's as romantic as he gets." Connie declared. "I've been telling him I'm not happy for two years. He acts like I'm talking about vacuuming or something. I'm sick of it. Now I'm thinking of leaving."

At the end of the first session Connie got around to saying she thinks she is having an "emotional relationship" with a person at work. "Nothing personal" Connie said. "I call Dick and ask for help with work issues and he always answers even if it is on the weekend."

What's going on here? Ryan has not changed. Nothing has changed in Connie's life except her thoughts. Connie has slowly but surely realized that she needs attention and the feeling of connection. She wants more than a body that appears once or twice a month.

**IMMEDIATE SOLUTION:** For Connie the first order of business is making a decision about her marriage. Quit dreaming about your emotional affair. Unless you are out of your marriage and can spend time with Dick he is a figment of your imagination and, as such, possesses wonderful, probably unreal qualities, while thoughts about your husband are negative.

An immediate need is to talk to your husband, let him know how unhappy you are and make an appointment for marriage counseling

**LONG TERM SOLUTION:** Get real. Connie is dreaming. As difficult as it is, Connie must return to the real world and deal with her marriage. As best she can, Connie is to imagine life without her husband and that means financially, socially, daily interactions and habits. Connie wants her husband to conveniently disappear while life goes on as usual and, in the meantime, she develops new relationships.

Examining the source of Connie's unhappiness is important and that means counseling. Also, Connie's husband needs a serious wake up call since he seems to be out of the equation. He may not be aware that the marriage is in jeopardy.

## TRAIN THE BRAIN

When you have a particular thought, day after day as Connie has had, you are effectively rewiring a part of your brain whether you intend to or not. This is true at mental and the physical level. For example, piano practice produces brain changes whether rehearsal is physical or mental.

Research shows that the brain is affected with either mental or physical rehearsal! Merely thinking about how to play tennis affects the brain's complicity in these skills just as does actual practice. While learning takes place at a rapid rate in the young, the cortical and other areas change throughout life and can be directed, by "intention" to change in desired ways. If what you want is dependant on brain function, focus and work toward your desire on a continuous basis and the brain will modify.

Happy relationships are fueled by positive, pleasurable behaviors and interactions. Unhappiness is neglect and disconnection with twisted interactions or deceit in its myriad forms.

Another arena that contains multiple possibilities for deceit is the Internet, where committed individuals often innocently check out interesting Internet sites. If, at that moment in time, the partnership happens to be rocky, an Internet site meant to add zing instead becomes a secret life. Chapter Six demystifies the role of divisive Internet issues.

## CHAPTER SEVEN

# I AM JUST NOT HAPPY...I'VE DISCOVERED MY PARTNER HAS INTERNET SECRETS

### INTERNET

The Internet touches all of our lives in many concrete, positive ways: access to data, e-mail, a writing tool, financial storage, games, and for singles, dating possibilities. Internet connections also have potential for relationship trouble when curiosity and loneliness spur secret Net explorations.

### DENISE AND CHRIS: BOREDOM AND THE INTERNET

Chris was *just not happy*, something was wrong at home but he could not seem to pin point the problem. Possible reasons buzzed around on the edges of his awareness and then, clarification. Chris uncovered Denise's secret Internet life.

### THERAPY

Denise and Chris are an interesting looking couple. Chris, 31, has a square, solid, powerful build; Denise, 29, has a round, nicely shaped body. Chris is as fair skinned and blonde as Denise is Latino, black hair and brown eyes. Denise is bright-eyed and bushy-tailed, eager to begin talking where Chris is watchful and quiet. He reacts and responds slowly although, uncharacteristically, Chris did set up their first counseling session.

After gathering preliminary information I said, "What brings you in?" Denise looked at Chris, waited a few seconds and then replied, "We are unhappy. We just cannot talk."

In marriage counseling, communication is generally a huge problem. Couples avoid talking about feelings, argue instead of talking, speak with an attitude or are fearful of saying the wrong thing. Denise tells me that they were able to communicate once upon a time, in fact, they talked like magpies, but a disconnect occurred early on, and winding their way back to interest and excitement with one another has never occurred.

I explained to Chris and Denise that their immediate disconnect experience is critical information for therapy but I also need an historical, individual chronological map of their marriage and background.

Evidently, while I was revealing the necessary background outline Chris whipped up his courage. He interrupted and leaned forward, "Excuse me, but before we start into our history I think you should know what precipitated my call to you. On Sunday I confronted Denise.

"Denise is having an Internet sex chat with a male co-worker. I don't know what to call it and I don't know if that's all it is, or if it's a full blown affair." Chris fell back on the couch.

Silence.

Denise appears horrified. Is she embarrassed and looking for my reaction? Turning to stare at Chris, Denise barks, "What are you talking about? I told you I have no interest in Jim."

Continuing to look at me Chris said, "Come on, Denise. I have copies of everything that you and Jim have discussed. I am sick every day that it goes on. With a co-worker, are you nuts? What do you want? Do you want a divorce?" Chris's face is red and one hand is shaking.

"All right, I admit I was wrong. I'm sorry." Denise's tone is agitated rather than imploring. Turning to me

Denise states, "I told Chris last night I made a mistake. I won't do it again, but he doesn't listen. He's making a huge deal out of it. I do not want to fight with him again. We had a monstrous fight last night—no, nothing physical.

Chris interjected, "You don't call throwing things physical?"

Denise continued, "Well, I mean we didn't physically hit one another. Chris never listens to me. He's in his own world and I suppose that's why this happened. I really don't know what possessed me—talk on the Net is so stupid.

"I tried to defend myself last night. I'm lonely and Chris knows it. He is up and gone at the crack of dawn. It's late when he gets home and he's exhausted, he falls asleep and that's it. Or, he's traveling.

"I feel like I don't have a marriage, no one's home. I mean no connection mentally or physically but right now what upsets me more than anything else is that Chris has known about this Internet situation for several weeks and he never said anything. If he cared about me he would have confessed instead of sneaking around and copying emails."

Ah, Denise that was clever, Chris is now the villain. Denise is bored, feels unloved, abandoned and because she has talked to Chris many times about her feelings, she is mad and blames him for her behavior.

Denise fuels her thoughts with boredom rationale. Stuck on a plateau, disinclined to act on her own, dissatisfied with her life and longing for the attention of a person with a one-track workaholic mind, she has put her happiness in Chris's hands and his hands are closed.

Chris does not show emotions other than anger and he certainly cannot tolerate an implication from Denise that he is responsible for her bad feelings. If Denise plays the emotion card Chris does not hear or understand or react. He shuts down and goes away either mentally or physically or both.

If sexual Internet talk is an unconscious stratagem to get Chris's attention, it worked. Denise's Internet liaison seems to have shattered his tough-guy façade and the impression he has of himself as a tough, stoic, hard-driving businessman who can take whatever life has to offer and throw it right back, in spades.

## FACING THE FACTS

Denise and Chris are now face to face with one another's character issues. It is difficult in any close relationship to really look at interaction evidence and understand the implications, especially when the evidence is not to your liking. Denise has chosen a distant person and since they married she has been in the business of trying to turn Chris into a loving, thoughtful homebody—which has not worked.

Denise says, "I don't want to change Chris. It's just that this is not the person I started out with." Where did he go? She thinks if she keeps chipping away the real Chris will emerge.

Denise thinks that Chris "should" know she needs attention. He does not. She thinks about the relationship. He does not. If he cared he would listen and understand her feelings. He does not. And from Denise's perspective all this is evidence that he did not take the information seriously or that he does not care.

Since Denise is the unhappy person, the only way she can get through Chris's concrete thinking is to delineate exactly what she needs. Let him know how many minutes of talk, how many minutes of touching, how often she desires sex and how many social situations are necessary.

Chris has been out of the relationship loop with a lopsided emphasis on his career. He has steered clear of emotional issues and kept his own feelings out of consciousness for most of his life. Now he's done a one-eighty; he always feels emotional and his wife is always on his mind.

Since Chris's career M.O. is problem solver/trouble shooter, he handles issues that are either concrete or he makes them concrete by deciding "yes", "no", "stop", or "start". Chris tells people what to do. He cannot tell Denise what to do; she won't listen. She simply tells him what to do and where he can go. Chris is swimming in a sea of emotional chaos, which is making him physically sick.

As a child Chris learned that males in his family did not tolerate emotional displays. If he was weepy he was told, "Knock it off or I'll give you something to cry about," or more sympathetically, "Big boys don't cry." The message was the same, feelings are not acceptable but his stoic style is no longer working.

**IMMEDIATE PROBLEM:** Establish a basis for trust and understanding. If these two are going forward Denise and Chris need to drop their defenses and be real. As it is, they are on high alert, afraid to let their guard down, fearful of being hurt or vulnerable.

The marriage may end if Chris is simply reacting to his wounded ego and not interested in listening to the marital issues Denise is experiencing. When Denise cloaks herself in her defensive attitude Chris may not find an entryway to her heart.

**IMMEDIATE SOLUTION:** Chris is in a state of shock. Since Chris is a black and white thinker, he requires pragmatic answers but he also needs to listen and, if possible, show empathy for Denise without being punitive.

Denise has Chris's attention. Chris shifted from a work-a-holic to a Denise-a-holic. On a daily basis, maybe morning noon and night, Denise has to be crystal clear that she is done with her on-line sex chat person. It is imperative that she drops the defensive attitude, the in-your-face tone and stance.

**LONG TERM SOLUTION:** Although both Chris and Denise are shaken by the Internet fiasco their desire to remain together appears to be cavalier, which may be a historical fear of being vulnerable, exacerbated by the Internet issue.

Whether Denise and Chris decide to forge ahead with their marriage or not, their inner life needs attention. As individuals they are floundering. Who are they and what do they want for their life?

Chris lives outside in; he is one-dimensional, reacting to career needs while avoiding relationship experiences and self-expansion. Wham! Distress has taken over and Chris is sick with stomachaches, diarrhea, back pain, headaches, depression and anxiety. His emotions, which are not being expressed in the relationship, found a place to dock—his body.

Is Denise better off? She expresses, screams, yells, throws things and takes action but her problem is not solved, instead she chose a shallow, destructive path.

The Internet crisis, if they choose to accept the challenge, has provided an opportunity to stop, focus on both their individual inner lives and their deeper needs in the relationship.

## A BAD MARRIAGE IS A MENTAL AND PHYSICAL HEALTH HAZARD

The health issues Chris experienced may have been genetically dormant, but certainly were exacerbated by stress in his marriage. A 2004 study tracked 72 married couples for 3 years to measure the effect marital stress had on health. Individuals in marriages with high levels of stress were more likely to have serious heart problems whereas those in happy marriages had fewer fatal accidents, lower rates of depression and suicide, less acute and chronic illness, and less susceptibility to alcohol abuse. Relationship problems have ominous mental and physical consequences.

## USING THE INTERNET TO RUIN YOUR RELATIONSHIP

Misuse of the Internet is a very modern way to disturb a relationship. For example, Bill phoned for a marriage counseling appointment stating that his marriage needed "tweaking." He said that he and his wife have been married eight years and, "Although we get along well and enjoy one another's company, we do have a variety of problems that need fixing."

And then he asked an interesting question. "Do you have any trouble working with men?" I said, "Why do you ask?" He kind of fumbled around and finally said, "Well, I was afraid you might side with my wife since you are female."

Bill is clever to put me on guard, in effect, "Be nice to me," and, at the same time, gender prejudice is a reasonable fear.

Because Bill and his wife Alice work long hours our appointment was in the evening when both should have been tired. Instead they were revved up and eager to tell their story, stumbling over one another to talk. Both Bill and Alice are 33, have demanding careers and present themselves in an alert, poised manner. Both claim their interest in separating is negative. In fact, they have recently built a house that they love.

Alice is nice looking, conservatively dressed and soft-spoken. Bill has graying red hair, a sales professional's presentation, somewhat flamboyant with lots to say.

After introductions and before I could ask, Alice, visibly upset, began by saying, "The reason we're here is that I saw something on the computer that shocked me. I seldom use our home computer, mainly because I work on a computer all day so even looking at the home computer translates to work.

"I digress. Last Thursday Bill was working late and it so happened that I had to connect with my office via computer. There had been a glitch at work that I won't go in to.

"When I brought up the screen I was face to face with a good looking blonde. Naturally I checked it out a little more and the blonde turned out to be part of a dating network. I was shocked. Even though no one was around I could feel my face flushing, my heart pounding, I don't know what else was happening because I couldn't think. My brain stopped. What in the world had Bill been doing on a Web dating page?

"Of course, I thought to myself, he is unhappy with me and is looking for a way out of the marriage or, at least, a diversion. At that moment divorce was the answer for me.

"I was devastated. The minute Bill walked in the door I jumped on him. I was upset; I wanted answers. He said he had no idea where the picture came from, where the site came from and he was as shocked as I was."

By now Alice was crying, "Well, how could he be innocent? He dashed to the computer, erased the site, shut down the Internet, closed the computer and then we started arguing in earnest. Right up to walking into your office he denies any involvement. Why did he shut down the computer? That doesn't make sense to me. Why didn't he start checking it out if he's innocent, as he pretends? I think he's lying."

Bill had been sputtering, trying to get a word in while Alice talked. His chance came and he quickly changed the subject, "I'm glad we're here. We've got a lot more problems than the Internet as far as I'm concerned.

"Alice won't kiss me. Can you believe that? Since we married she won't kiss. I need hugging, kissing and affection." (He was too timid to say sex at this point.)

"She's got an anger problem," nodding at Alice. "She comes home from work and starts in with me sometimes about something as simple as setting the table wrong."

In a little different tone, "Naturally she has to vent to me. Who else?

"Alice's family is not supportive. Her father is a liar." Turning to Alice, "Alice will tell you that's true." Alice nods agreement. "Her sister, well, that's another story."

(Now we discover that Alice is faced with a suspected lying husband after living life with a lying father.)

"Not that my family is wonderful. My father was an alcoholic. I left home at 16 and had to figure out how to survive but I only see my family once or twice a year. We have to have dinner with her dad every Saturday and I just hate the way he treats Alice."

Alice interjected, "My dad is 81 and lives five miles away. Bill's family is on the other side of town."

Bill continues and while talking he continuously looks at Alice, pats her arm, nods at her implying he needs agreement. "Alice lived at home until she was 25. I don't know how she survived mentally with that father. He tells ridiculous stories and makes outrageous statements which you can't refute because he is a lying nut case." Bill pats Alice and nods and again she doesn't disagree when he talks about her father. "He just drives me crazy."

It sounds like Bill is getting his ducks in order, his defense ready, before heading into the issue of the Internet. Bill is hoping that the Internet becomes a non-issue since there is no evidence that he has been anything but reliable and truthful.

With each succeeding therapy session Alice is calmer about Bill and the Internet dating issue. Since Alice is a computer person she knows how to retrieve lost computer material and so far her frantic search for evidence has been unproductive and Bill's position continues to be one of innocence, pointing out that sites simply pop up.

Alice's sudden realization that her peaceful life disappeared with a glance at her computer is like being hit by a truck. Shocked out of her habitual thought patterns Alice's discovery translated to feeling unloved and unsure of herself.

Although she reports tearful, fearful days, she is focusing on improving the marriage and firming her ego by taking charge of cranky, angry feelings and making a concerted effort to be affectionate.

Bill was shaken when Alice pointed out his "failings." Plopped in a chair until Alice arrived and made dinner, Bill expected her to be the cleaning lady, shopping person and cook even though she drove an hour longer back and forth from work. Alice played her part in that scenario by doing the cooking and cleaning then feeling put out and mad.

In therapy Alice and Bill figured out how to safely talk about feelings, set up an evenly distributed house schedule, and essentially eliminated ongoing, nagging problems that had caused daily unhappiness.

The Internet dating issue was never entirely clarified but Alice decided she had gone as far as she could go with her investigations and decided to put the issue aside.

## INTERNET DOUBLECROSS

What if you turned on the computer and saw your wife or husband's face staring out at you?

When I lifted the phone I barely had an opportunity to say, "Hello", before I heard a story similar to Alice and Bill's, "I'm desperate for help. I seldom use my home computer simply because I'm on the computer all day at work, I work long hours and am sick of it by the time I get home. My wife knows that and now I think she counts on the fact that I seldom turn it on.

"Yesterday I wanted to check out a friend's web site and when I turned on the computer I was shocked! A sexual scene with my wife's face appeared. I practically went into cardiac arrest. I confronted my wife and she acted surprised. She said she hadn't the vaguest notion where that came from and she was upset because I thought the picture was real.

"I'm in a rage and feel crazed but I don't know what to do. I do not want to tell anyone about this just in case there's a chance it's a fluke. Of course, mainly I think she's lying to me.

"My wife refuses to see a marriage counselor but I have to talk confidentially about this situation. Can I come in tonight?"

When Brian arrived in my office he was obviously agitated. The first order of business was to help Brian express his feelings, calm down and, second, to take a look at possibilities.

## AFTER THE SHOCK:

It is possible that the dating site was an accident but, let's look at the worst possible scenario, the *If's*:

If your wife left this information in clear sight we can assume that she is sending an unconscious message. This is the message: Warning! Our relationship is dangerously slipping and sliding and may be headed toward extinction.

If your wife is a person given to lies and deceit her plan is to cheat both you and the dating partner.

If true, your wife is a philanderer and the sooner you recognize that fact, the better.

If you discover the Internet is being used as a dating link, pornography or for any suspicious reasons take these actions (ideally before confronting your partner).

## IMMEDIATE SOLUTION:

1.  Check your computer for tell-tale information:
    a.  Click on History; sometimes even erased cookies will still be there.
    b.  Use common sense (if a number of cookies pop up be suspicious, not one or two).
    c.  Click on Address and scroll down arrow.
2.  Record computer information, web site, etc.
3.  Print and copy all information.
4.  Check for other connections: chat rooms, other dating services or pornographic sites.

The Internet has stopped you in your tracks and given you the opportunity to experience your marriage from a different perspective. That is the good news but may be the bad news as well.

If you are married to a liar, which was the end result with Brian's Internet dilemma, and if you choose to stay married, the rest of your life will be mired in questions and confusion.

## STOP PRETENDING

This is your life and when you pretend your behavior or your partner's behavior does not have consequences you are lying to yourself. If an Internet issue occurred in a business setting what would happen? Think: If I were the CEO and needed this person in the company exactly what would I say and how would I follow up?

Sit down for a talk with your spouse. Having thought through exactly what you want to say and in a business-like, non-threatening tone, present your understanding of the Internet issues and what you desire from this moment forth. Then do not argue. Listen.

If it appears that your spouse did not hear you or is proceeding as though you had not spoken. No problem. You repeat the same exact words the next day. After three repeats with no response in behavior or conversation take seriously the fact that your partner is ignoring you, is going to continue doing what she has been doing and now, the crucial issue, what do you do?

You are going to change your tactics. You are not going to let the issue either disappear into thin air or fearfully argue without a solution.

## COMPUTER FEARS

To allay computer fears when there have been any suspicious happenings on the computer, check them out. The idea of talking to or confronting your partner about your questions is tempting—but will not provide information. One in a thousand guilty people are going to say, "Yes. I was interested in dating sites."

Do not confront your partner until you get information. This is very difficult advice to follow because you feel compelled to talk about your distress and you want your partner to know you are not stupid. If your mate tells you he is searching the Internet for a date, then what? Will you accept the admission and be happy that he is an honest person who in some convoluted way is trying to maintain the marriage? No way.

If your spouse lives a secret life, now is the time to face it. Do not pretend you did not see what you saw. Do not accept, "I can't imagine where that came from. It's one of those emails that simply pop up from nowhere." No. Your partnership is in trouble. If you choose to ignore the message or believe your partner, you are acting in and pretending all is well. All is not well.

As best you can, control your wild emotions and thoughts. Do not struggle for the truth with your partner. Instead, inundate your mind with the fact that the Internet is your friend and has provided an opportunity to stop and seriously look at yourself, your husband or wife and what you want in this marriage. Your suspicious thoughts and what the evidence produces may be very different.

Although this sounds ridiculous, an ugly Internet surprise can be the beginning of a new, interesting, exciting partnership. The possibility of loss alerts you to the importance of your partner. From my book *Affairs: Emergency Tactics*: "People in relationships become sloppy in their treatment of one another; disregarding, demanding, disrespecting, treating partners unlike the friends they were during courtship. Too often, partners act as though a good relationship is their birthright and become angry if things don't go their way."

## STOP OLD BEHAVIOR AND MAKE CHANGES

**You** stop ruminating now. This is the only day you have, the only minute you have. Try something different for 10 minutes. In the middle of a marital crisis you can alter your thoughts and find relief.

Thoughts are things. Thoughts change the nuances in your face, change your tone of voice and ultimately alter words you speak. Thoughts change your physiology. When your thoughts are stressful your body takes a hit: heart rate changes, blood pressure rises, breathing accelerates. If stress continues you will experience back pain, exhaustion, stomach cramps, diarrhea, as well as other symptoms and, if stress continues, you will experience chronic physical problems.

Thoughts are powerful.

**Ten minutes a day** can change your marriage. Find a time, 10 AM, 3 PM, 8:30 PM, and focus 10 minutes completely, totally on your partner. Your partner has positive qualities that you like or love. Pretend your partner is someone you are in awe of, look up to and respect with your whole heart. Do not let negative thoughts creep in.

Plan on **resistance** from yourself. Your mind will be oppositional and fragmented, jumping from a positive focus to why you cannot and should not bother. Resistance includes these thoughts:

1. Putting different thoughts in my mind is ridiculous.
2. My spouse will not see a difference.
3. He is the problem, not me.
4. I cannot change my thoughts; they just come to mind. What am I supposed to do? Are you suggesting I spend time thinking about my thoughts when I have a serious problem with my partner?
5. This therapist does not know what she is talking about.
6. I don't have time.
7. What about me? Who thinks about me?

## OPPOSITIONAL THINKING

We have our addict-like thinking, fragmented and oppositional, which in marriage spikes from love to fear, pleasure to displeasure. By fragmented thinking I mean our natural propensity to entertain opposites. We rotate back and forth with oppositional thoughts: "That's it, I'm getting a divorce!" Later, "Well, it's not so bad. I'm better off than other people." The fragmented mind allows a variety of ideas to be introduced into your thinking repertoire. It could be considered an inquiring mind. That is the plus. The minus is confusion, indecision and fear.

When you ask yourself, "Why should I change? Shouldn't my partner change as well?" Yes. That would be ideal. However, you are the only one with control over you; you know you cannot change another person. You have been trying for years to help your partner understand your truth, the real experience, the way things truly are, but for some reason your partner has his own point of view and tries to help you understand his perception of life and his problems.

In other words, if you choose to stay with this partner, just like looking at a computer template that is unchanging, you know what to expect. A different personality will not suddenly appear.

Instead, decrease unhappiness for ten minutes, soothe and center yourself. How do you do that when you are trapped in an unhappy relationship? This is how: *Recognize your oppositional thinking, take charge, change your thoughts and, given what is, decide how to proceed.*

Thinking is the battery charge that fuels emotion and behavior. Emotion and behavior are the result of ongoing, instantaneous reactive, often unconscious, thought processes. Your history and defense system developed an unconscious ego-protecting mental check list to assess how you feel, to analyze why you feel the way you do, and, in case you are distressed, to assign blame or to understand the problem.

The next section focuses on unhappiness generated by another level of discomfort that is seldom concrete, in other words, you can't quite put your finger on the exact problem.

# SECTION TWO

## Defensive Avoidance

So far we've dealt with obvious issues that generate unhappiness. However, when you are unhappy with your relationship and cannot point to a specific problem, then what?

When you can't quite put your finger on the problem you may be living unhappily with an underlying issue of defensive avoidance, difficult to define and for that exact reason, impossible to solve.

Chapters Eight, Nine and Ten examine different aspects of defensive avoidance where our defense system attempts to protect us from painful, anxious feelings by repressing conflicts. Subconscious defensive avoidance styles (passive, passive aggressive or impulsive) retard relationship connection and divert communication from clarity and decision-making.

## CHAPTER EIGHT

# I'M JUST NOT HAPPY...MY PARTNER IS PASSIVE

### DEFENSIVE AVOIDANCE

It is all well and good to talk about taking charge of unhappiness by changing behavior but for much of the day we are on automatic pilot, reacting to spouses and others through the porous screen of our defense system.

Hidden from consciousness, meant to guard the ego and protect us from anxiety and emotional harm, defense mechanisms interpret situations, communication and emotion before they reach consciousness. At the same time that defenses unconsciously protect us from painful and anxious feelings, they often cause interpersonal difficulty by avoiding real connection and intimacy.

We all have defenses that occasionally creep into conversations but there are people whose primary communication style is defensive and offensive at the same time.

The following defenses do not find truth in their partner's point of view; instead they argue and defend their own positions which include:

1. Always being right
2. Blaming others
3. Being the victim
4. Denying feelings but acting out: pouting, withdrawing, being sullen, stomping around
5. Saying "I'm awful" or "I'm wrong"
6. Never acknowledging the problem

7.   Being the educator - the "know-it-all"
8.   Thinks he or she is perfect
9.   Using sarcasm
10.  Being jolly or laughing inappropriately

We need our defense mechanisms to ward off the real or imaginary slings and arrows of life, and, in particular, the ego vulnerability exposed in an intimate relationship, but you can see by the list above that defenses often bristle with hostility and prevent clear communication. The defense that is meant as a screen to protect the ego is instead a guard wall, keeping love and happiness away.

Any idea that you can simply point out your partner's defensive style and she has an "ah-hah" experience will not work. You need concrete words and non-confrontational methods to present your interpretation of his or her defenses or the conversation will turn ugly. And before you point out your spouse's defensive style it is important to know in what way you are defensive and be fully prepared to manage right-back-at-cha attack talk.

## DEFENSES THAT MULTIPLY UNHAPPINESS

Defensive avoidance includes aggressive, impulsive words and behavior, or evasive passive or passive aggressive avoidance styles that shift you automatically away from your partner. Defensive styles:

1. Passive
2. Passive Aggressive
3. Impulsive

See if you recognize any of your own or your partner's defensive positions:

## THE PASSIVE STYLE

Defined by *Miriam Webster's Dictionary*, passive means that you are "submissive, influenced or acted upon without exerting influence," which means that you go along with your partner no matter what. If it is o.k. with him, it is o.k. with you. No opinions, no ideas, nobody is home. "You" have disappeared.

When you follow the passive, habitual mind track you are being bullied by life. You have learned to accept your own style no matter what. You are a martyr. Or, you have thought it out and the consequences scare you into submission.

Passive or cowardice pain is like a toothache that pushes on the nerve and never leaves. You are shut down, in psychic pain, and you have learned to live with it. You may not realize it but passive pain is a choice. You put yourself in pain by carefully nurturing your fear thoughts and taking control by locking in your passive stance.

## MARY AND DICK

Mary and Dick had an unwritten marital contract. Her role was to be the perfect, passive wife, content with her husband's decisions. Nothing was discussed seriously unless it was from Dick's understanding of the world. He made pronouncements and Mary went along—until Florida.

At age 55 Dick suddenly decided he was sick of his managerial position, sick of the climate in Michigan and needed to change his life and move to Florida. Mary protested—weakly as usual—and as Mary said when she called from Florida to make an appointment, "Before I knew it we had quickly packed up everything and left our children, grandchildren, friends and family."

In her first therapy session Mary, a 54-year-old housewife, barely sat down before she started quietly expressing powerful, negative feelings. "I hate Florida. When we settled in Florida I realized I hate my husband. I feel like I want to scream obscenities at him, which isn't like me at all. I don't even swear."

## WHAT HAPPENED TO MARY?

Dick may have been sick of Michigan but Mary was in psychic shock when she realized what she had done. She had jumped up, moved and left everything and everyone she cared about. Mary felt completely at Dick's mercy. Mary said, "I can't stand the way he talks to me. He's always annoyed, snappy, barking at me and adamant about his point of view."

Mary said she fell deeper and deeper into depression and blamed Dick, telling him he only thought of himself. Dick was shocked. He considered himself a considerate, loving husband and could not believe that his wife thought of him as a tyrant.

The trauma produced a crisis that Mary could not ignore. In therapy Mary examined herself and her life and found that she has a right to express her opinions, she has a position and one of them is "I hate Florida and I need to move back to Michigan." Her years of a passive martyr position, watching, waiting and avoiding confrontations no longer worked.

Mary has spent her life trying to please her husband and do whatever he wanted as though what she wanted did not matter, or, more likely, she did not matter. As Mary talked about her passivity she realized she was a participant in what had happened. She played the victim and since Dick was the assertive, aggressive person he was the responsible party for events in their life. When Mary did have a point of view instead of asserting herself she spoke tentatively, questioningly, like a little girl.

Mary is at a pivotal point in her life where the Florida move may be a blip in her life or the beginning of an alteration and shift in Mary's defense mechanisms, an opening for Mary to crawl through and find out who she is.

**IMMEDIATE SOLUTION:** Continue to speak your mind. Do not fall back into letting your spouse or partner take responsibility for both your lives. Now that you have outted yourself to yourself, you need to stay out. Check out these passive behaviors:

Here is what you do:
1. Give up directing your mind.
2. Surrender to the moment.
3. Dissociate or blank out.
4. Oh no. I can't stand this but fearfully stay rooted to the spot.
5. Make your partner the king, while you are the helpless subject.
6. Make excuses, "I have to go to the bathroom." "I'm late." "I have to get some sleep." Any of these may be true. However, if the issue is not later discussed, the excuses are bogus.

Look at your passive methods and be specific, exactly what is the behavior that shuts down communication? Begin a campaign with yourself to consciously stamp out your "natural" silent reactions and replace them with words and actions. Instead of raising your defensive bar higher when your partner suggests that you are being defensive, acknowledge your defensiveness, explain what you are experiencing or, more importantly, listen and, as difficult as it is, let the information dock in your brain.

**LONG TERM SOLUTION:** Living with a passive person is like living with a wet noodle. A passive person mentally slinks away from reality, acting like a coward. If you are a passive person, get into therapy and stay there until you know why you are so fearful.

Passivity is a method of hiding yourself while you point the finger at your partner either in your mind or in your behavior, "There he goes again. He knows everything. I'm always wrong," or you distastefully move away and make sure your body language suggests censure. A disgusted look, shrug, tossing hair or head, pursing lips, rolling the eyes, any of these quick responses indicates that you are dismayed or even appalled.

Listen to yourself. You know when you are simply going along without verbalizing a point of view. Force yourself to state your position. What is the worst that can happen? Your partner will disagree, be verbally aggressive or discount your position.

If you want to stay stuck, fine. But be honest with yourself. You are getting something out of the present situation. By your acceptance you let your partner know that there is no reason for him to change.

Mary and Dick are working on change and struggling. Intellectual knowledge and concretely knowing what to do is one thing, turning that information into a life style is another. But, once you know something you cannot not know it. It will take time but I think Mary and Dick have a relationship that is on an upward trajectory and happiness is within reach.

While living with or being a passive person produces unhappiness, there are other hidden defense mechanisms that result in mysterious, serious discontent. Chapter Eight describes how to define and deal with a passive-aggressive person.

## CHAPTER NINE

# I'M JUST NOT HAPPY...MY PARTNER WILL NOT TAKE ACTION

### DEFENSIVE AVOIDANCE: THE PASSIVE AGGRESSIVE POSITION

The second defensive avoidance position is passive-aggressive: You are passive in words and deeds. However, you refuse to acquiesce. You simply listen, act like you are in agreement, conveniently forget or procrastinate and then aggressively proceed to do whatever you want to do.

### RANDY: PASSIVE AGGRESSIVE

The perfectly balanced pair: An accountant, Debbie, and a social worker, Randy. Debbie is orderly, conventional and non-emotional except when she is mad at Randy. Randy verbalizes feelings, makes messes around the house, procrastinates and "forgets" plans.

Married 23 years with the kids grown and out of the house, they are nose to nose with one another. Where personality issues had been on the periphery of their partnership in the past, now their differences feel unbearable. Still, both agree they love one another and want to continue the marriage.

Randy called for marriage counseling and said, "We have done marriage counseling twice before so you could say we are jaded. We probably aren't good candidates for counseling, but we just don't know what else to do. We constantly butt heads and spend our days upset."

Sometimes people are not ready for emotional change. Their intellect tells them the relationship is in shambles but their emotions trail behind kicking and screaming wanting to continue old behaviors. Or, they are scared and truly believe divorce is imminent. The other possibility is - and this is hard to believe - they get so much out of being miserable that misery is difficult to give up.

## DEBBIE

Debbie is a 47-year old, tiny, five-foot dynamo, practically twitching and eager to get the counseling show on the road. Randy is a 46-year old bear of a man who talks slowly, looks like Mr. Out-Doors in corduroy pants, boots and plaid jacket.

After getting family background information and each person's version of their marital history, Debbie began with her "real" problem, "I get so tired of trying to talk to Randy. Half the time he doesn't respond, he just stares at me, or I catch him glancing at the newspaper or TV while I'm talking. And it's not like I talk on and on. We barely have five minutes a day together. Then I begin to get mad at him and then, of course, he won't talk to me. Or, he agrees he will do whatever and then never does it." She added as a way of softening the sound of anger, "This is just my perspective."

Randy's perspective naturally was different. "I never say the right thing. I know something's wrong with me when it comes to having a serious talk with Debbie. I'm inept. I not only can't carry on a conversation I become too emotional and that drives Debbie crazy."

Randy said, "For example, Tuesday Debbie said she wanted to contact a couple we hadn't seen for a while and have them over. That was fine with me. But somehow she started to get upset with me because I didn't join in with planning the evening and when she does that I just feel myself shut down. I guess I zone out, can't even hear her."

Debbie jumped in, "Instead of Randy saying, 'Sounds good' or 'No, I don't want to see them' he just stares at me. I know I start pressing. I feel like I can't just go ahead and make plans without consulting him first so when he acts like he's not interested or is out to lunch when I'm talking, I'm upset. He might just decide to go to our cabin up North and I'll be left holding the bag. He's done that before.

"I guess I don't do what I want. I keep waiting to see what he wants—but he never tells me. Or, if we do plan something he conveniently forgets."

"Randy says he will do something, like a chore around the house, and I think he means to take care of it, but I have to keep nagging and even then I end up doing most things. He drives me crazy."

While Debbie is talking Randy is acting exactly as Debbie described his behavior, staring at her, and then in his defense he says, "I'm considered an expert with other people's problems but with Debbie I can't do anything right. I don't know what to say. I'm not excited about having people over but if she wants to have company that's fine. I don't know why she expects me to jump up and down and then when I don't, she gets angry."

## THE DAMAGING DANCE OF PASSIVE AGRESSION

Randy passively plays, 'Woe is me; I am a leaf in the wind. My wife's words decide my feelings,' but then proceeds to do whatever he wants to do whether he has indicated he is in agreement or not. And Debbie sets herself up by preparing to be mad if he doesn't respond as he 'should' and is continually frustrated by his "say this and do that" behavior. This is their avoidance dance.

Debbie and Randy have danced this dance so many times before they know exactly how it will end. They really know how to solve the problem: Be definitive. Debbie might simply say she is going to ask friends over or Randy can indicate the plan is fine with him, instead they refuse to rewrite their history while pretending to themselves the situation is out of control.

## HISTORY

Debbie is the oldest in a family where father was mean-spirited, a critical boss, and mother was wimpy and clingy. Debbie identified with the aggressor - her father - and was the mouthy, active kid who received verbal abuse without a mother to protect her.

Although in most areas Debbie takes charge and has chosen a pliable husband (like her mother), she treats her husband as though he carries a whip (like her father) while expecting him to take charge, despite contrary evidence.

Randy grew up in a family where his father was gone most of the time but when he was home he was harsh and particularly brutal with Randy, one of five children. Randy's method of managing his father was to leave the house and wander in the woods; he learned to avoid possible problems that he could not solve.

When we are children we have to find methods to manage difficult situations and as a rule those defenses follow us into adulthood. Ultimately, as in Debbie and Randy's situation, learned childish defenses are just that, childish. Hardened into rigidity even when the methods don't work, Debbie and Randy cannot wiggle into new ways of being together.

## STOPPING THE INSANITY OF DEFENSIVENESS

**IMMEDIATE SOLUTION:** Debbie and Randy: Stop! Think! Defensiveness is not your friend so quit pretending that your act/react drama means anything. If you are serious enough to take time for counseling, you can seriously focus on getting what you want. These mind-stopping defenses helped you somewhere along your lifeline but are distressing now.

Debbie: If Randy does not react as you want him to, say to yourself, "So what!" and continue with your social plans. He will participate or not. Hire someone to help you around the house whether Randy objects or not. You have evidence that he wants to take care of chores, he plans to take care of chores but they do not get done.

Randy: When Debbie is upset or angry she has a right to her feelings. Let her have emotions. Acknowledge them, take her words seriously but do not personalize what you imagine her emotional experience is.

**LONG TERM SOLUTION, DEBBIE:** Fact: For years Randy has passively indicated he will take care of a chore or will participate in a social event. Fact: Time and time again chores are not completed and he may or may not be available to socialize. Since Randy does not take action his behavior appears passive. Whatever his words are his behavior says, "No" and that is aggressive.

1. You either are flat-lined and do not verbalize feelings, or you are irritable, which is off-putting and stops communication. Verbalize your frustration with specific words, directly and seriously.
2. Stop imagining that Randy will be different or should be different.
3. To continually expect your partner to be different is a set-up for upset. If you continue your expectations, ask yourself, "Why?" One obvious reason is that you do not want to accept what is real.
4. You know you cannot change Randy. The worst that can happen is that Randy will stay the same. Can you continue to tolerate his behavior?

**LONG TERM SOLUTION, RANDY:** You are well aware that saying one thing and doing another is bad behavior. Your passive aggressive defenses create conflict for you and are interfering with living a life of integrity. You may have good intentions but that means nothing when behavior does not match words.

Passive aggressive avoidance was functional as a child when you needed to protect yourself against inappropriate adult emotions. Procrastination is all about being a baby, "I don't feel like doing that right now and I won't!"

Seriously think about and decide what to do about these excuses and behaviors:

1. Relinquish responsibility for your own words.
2. Give up any effort to focus on solutions.
3. Bait and switch thoughts. Slide away from what needs to be done to an irrelevant thought, word or action.
4. Preoccupied. 'I meant to have a talk about what she said but I forgot, it slipped my mind.'
5. Dismiss your partner's words of distress.
6. Pretend confusion.

You have been unhappy with good reason. You have been deep into not paying attention to yourself, however, now you are asking for help. Behaviors that are recognized and acknowledged can be deliberately changed with focus and patience.

## AVOIDANCE AS A WAY TO DEEPEN THE PROBLEMS

When you live with a passive aggressive person constant frustration is your companion. Do not avoid what is real; alter those frustrated thoughts:

1. Review a familiar scenario and rework it like a play that needs editing. Imagine responding differently within and without.
2. Recognize cowardice. He is afraid to put his real thoughts and feelings on the line.
3. Can you react differently? Be realistic.
4. If you react differently what do you expect from your spouse?

You can alter responses. You may not be able to speak or act differently immediately. No problem. Perseverance is critical and this is where challenge rears its ugly head.

1. Think about one habitual interaction between you and your spouse where you butt heads. Keep it in mind and then...
2. Decide on one simple thought. It does not matter what the thought is. It can be 'think', 'stop', 'focus', anything that redirects your habit and consciousness takes over.
3. Make a pact with yourself. When that interaction occurs, stop and quiet your mind.
4. Do not in your mind or in fact react in the same old way.
5. Be a boy/girl scout and be prepared for all potentials.
6. If your partner comes up with something unexpected, you mull it over.
7. You do not have to act or react to everything.

We cling to the known; we love our old thoughts just like a baby loves its pacifier. There is a time for the baby to move on and give up the pacifier and there is a time for you to move on to conscious rethinking of your marriage. Passive aggressive behavior is juvenile.

On another rung of the juvenile, defensive ladder is the impulsive person who, just like a baby, feels free to act out any thought or emotion.

The next defensive avoidance position, impulsivity, is explained in Chapter Ten.

## CHAPTER TEN

# I'M JUST NOT HAPPY...MY PARTNER IS IMPULSIVE

### IMPULSIVITY

The third defensive avoidance position is impulsivity. As an impulsive person you do not want to hear what your partner thinks because it is wrong; it is not what you think and believe so you say or do the first thing that comes to mind.

Why do you so adamantly defend your point of view? You have learned that your spouse (i.e., parent) is not going to listen and understand you, so you ram your ideas into his head aggressively and stop him in his tracks.

An unstable environment can produce a child who identifies with the aggressor. Acting on emotion is paramount when a parent is abusive. The child learns to shut up or shout out to protect itself from a parent or siblings but instead of protection the child's psyche becomes the victim, vigilant and anxious in a life that is a mental quagmire without any rational solution to problems.

The acting-out child, now adult, solution to an impulsive thought is to take inappropriate action, which means that you do something verbally or physically to allay tension.

After you act out, your anxiety may increase a hundred fold because you are now the negative focus. You are psychologically trapped: If you do not act, you cannot stand the tension, but if you do act the problem is often magnified.

## IMPULSES GUARANTEE EMOTIONS

A premature return from a fun trip to Branson, Missouri prompted Ashly to call my office and ask for an appointment as quickly as possible. Her trip to Branson had ended in a marital emergency.

Two days later Ashly was in my office. While I gathered general information I heard sniffling and in a quivering voice Ashly asked for Kleenex.

Ashly said, "I took an early flight back, alone, after Keith and I had an argument. Keith's my husband. It was awful. He embarrassed me in front of a roomful of people and he wouldn't tell me what the problem was. In fact, it's been five days and he's still not talking. He knows that drives me crazy."

Wiping away tears Ashly said, "You won't believe what started it all—my cousin's husband told her why Keith was mad and she told me, of course—we were all at a country western bar when my husband asked me to dance. I said 'No' because the music sounded like a square dance.

"That's it! That's why he won't speak.

"Actually, that's how he is; he will just act on a whim. Two months ago he bought a new, very expensive truck even though he has a year-old truck. Never mentioned to me that he was even thinking of a new truck, and then he comes up with some ridiculous excuse for buying it. I am so upset when he does these things. I'm just flabbergasted because we've talked about being open with one another, especially about money, but when he wants something or feels something, Bingo! There isn't any conversation; he just does what he wants to do.

"He's not totally a jerk. In his defense I do have to say he's a wonderful father to Ryan, my eight-year old son, but it's like he's got all the power, like now, not speaking to me. He's the one who's wrong and I'm the one who suffers.

Of course, the definition of who is wrong depends on who is talking.

## ASHLY AND KEITH

Ashly's first therapy session was full of emotion, tears dripping down her cheeks, some sobs that she apologized for (apology not needed). She has a huge problem that appears unsolvable to her: What do you do with a person who is in a marriage but keeps thoughts and feelings to himself and, in the meantime, does whatever he wants?

My first thought was Ashly's choice. What unresolved issues resulted in Ashly's choice of an impulsive person who seems to have different values?

Ashly, who presents as an attractive, slim, 32-year old, blue-eyed, brown-haired, well-dressed female, was raised in a family of ultra-conservative parents who tend to be controlling. Since parental traits did not crop up recently, we know that Ashly grew up in a careful, perhaps fearful, environment where comfort for the family meant doing the right thing, saving money, never squandering time, being diligent, in other words, being responsible at all times.

Ashly had already made one move that shook the family. Divorce. Given her conservative family, divorce was a brave step. Ashly said her parents were so upset by the idea of divorce that they went through her divorce in worse emotional shape than she did.

Ashly's subsequent marital choice of an impulsive free spirit suggests that she is trying to disentangle herself vicariously from her family restrictions, but the desire to be free is at war with the straight and narrow path on which she was trained.

## BRANSON

Life is in the details. I asked Ashly what else was happening that night at the Branson country western bar and had anything untoward happened during their trip or before leaving home.

Well, it turns out that Keith's sister who is having money problems not only came to Branson with them, but she stayed in their hotel room to save money and Ashly spent a lot of vacation time with her.

Sounds like a disaster waiting to happen.

Me: Is it possible that your husband felt left out and jealous? Ashly's answer, "Yes, I think he was, but he shouldn't have been. I didn't dance with anyone except his sister."

Now we understand what happened in Branson. Although Ashly and Keith flew in together they were never alone. Quite possibly Keith had different ideas about their vacation, perhaps romantic/sexual ideas. We can see that if there had been a serious discussion between them in Branson or before hand, at home, about how they were going to handle an extra person, a happy ending would have been possible.

Nevertheless, understanding and changing the serious relationship disruption of silence, impulsive behavior and Ashly's part in their marital story is critical.

**IMMEDIATE SOLUTION:** When you live with an impulsive partner you are vigilant, wary, and fearful of their next inappropriate remark or behavior. If your partner is not diagnosable, that is, does not have either an impulsive personality disorder or manic personality disorder, different behavior on your part will absolutely change the relationship equation.

How about being as understanding to Keith as you would to a stranger? Rather than treating him with outrage, instead you indicate that you are puzzled, surprised and curious about what is going on with him.

Do not dramatically react to his words and behavior by chastising and showing disapproval. Your reaction further cements the dystonic relationship dance. Chances are good that the following reactions have had absolutely no positive effect in the past nor will they at this moment in time.

For example, either you think or say:

1. Why did you say that?
2. What's wrong with you?
3. How many times have we discussed your impulsive actions?
4. You act like a child and do whatever you want.
5. Why do you hurt my feelings by not talking to me before you act?

Or, you indicate your disapproval by a disgusted look, physically turning away or mentally shutting down.

It is difficult to control habitual reactions and every reaction listed above has become habitual. Catch and stop negative Keith thoughts.

The next suggestion is difficult. The suggestion will not seem like a solution. It is. The suggestion is difficult to put into operation because you have other negative emotional thoughts in your mind that feel impossible to ignore but—you can do it.

Why should you be the one doing all this work when he is the culprit? Why? Because it works.

Begin by practicing the law of substitution. With each thought that feeds the idea that your husband 'should not' act in particular ways substitute a positive idea such as, I love Keith, I am interested in how his mind works, Keith has wonderful attributes, Keith is a good father, Keith is a good provider. Use any or all of these ideas to alter your own thoughts. Constant negative thinking and words will not change Keith but your negative thinking is evident in tone, words and the nuances in your face.

Another substitution: Write down your difficulty with him, hold the problems up to the light of reason, dissect them, mull them over, then cut up the paper, burn it, put it in the garbage, throw it away.

When you say to yourself this will not work use powerful feeling words to tell yourself, negative reactions have not made a difference. When you are dialoguing with yourself summon up powerful feelings to make the point. I know it sounds like hocus-pocus but you have to make a statement to your brain or the dialogue is simply part of the 60,000 thoughts roaming through your mind.

You are going to change a few neurons in your brain. To change those neurons you monitor and discard old thoughts by catching reactions and muffling habitual words.

The trick is to keep your resolve. Ideas, as you know, have a way of slipping away. You will need sticky notes, messages in your planner, on your Ipod, or in your Blackberry. Mainly, you need the message stuck firmly in your brain.

React to his silence with silence. Again, as difficult as it is, keep your mouth shut; view silence as his tactic to control himself. Your silence is an aid to him.

When a moratorium is declared, the silence is over and the time is right, discuss with empathy your reaction to his withdrawal. You can tell him that you understand his need to keep himself under control but that you, of course, cannot read his mind and want to know his thoughts.

If he refuses to talk simply say you will talk about it another day—and three days later talk again. Do not be discouraged if that does not work, three days later bring up his silence again. You must talk with understanding, no anger, no snide comments, and no historical overview.

Why should you be the one to put in all the effort? This is your life. This is your husband. If you prefer a happy life with Keith you start the ball rolling. Serious efforts to understand and change the status quo reap huge rewards, particularly since Keith has declared his desire to please you.

**LONG TERM SOLUTION:** Keith is impulsive. At the same time he wants to please you, and I believe his impulsivity is also a problem to him since, particularly regarding money, he is defensive, backtracks, or plays the you-do-it-too card. (You buy clothes; you go on vacations.)

You chose an impulsive partner for good reason. The "I did not know he was this impulsive when I fell in love" makes no difference now.

It is important for you to recognize impulsiveness is a feature of his personality and your unhappiness will not make it go away nor will it help him work on control. Keith is defensive if you respond to him by chastising.

The overview of the relationship is that you and Keith are at opposite ends of the pole. You are conservative; he is liberal. These qualities can either balance the relationship or you live nervously watching and waiting for his next move. In that case you are a reactor rather than an actor in your own life.

Being an actor means you choose your thoughts; your thoughts direct your life. You will be vigilant, that is a part of you, but at the same time, think ahead.

Think about his excellent qualities such as why you love him and when a distracting impulse occurs, think of effective responses. Get rid of thoughts that tell you: 'He should not act that way; he shouldn't say those things; he's making me mad.'

You do not add happiness to your life with those ideas. You feel happy when you use your mind in positive ways to solve problems.

The next story, Kim and Jered, combines an impulsive and a passive person. Can this marriage be saved? Sometimes couples consciously desire change but unconsciously either they are unable or unwilling to take the steps necessary to change habitual thoughts and behavior.

Often the definition of a particular defensive avoidance position is not played out in life exactly as defined. The purity of the defense is gone and instead there is a mix and match of defenses. This was the case for Kim, who is passive, and Jerod, who is aggressive and impulsive.

## KIM AND JEROD

Kim reports that she has finally had enough. She said on the phone, "I think the marriage is really over but I want to check out all options."

Kim came to the office January 2, right after the holidays. Kim's daughters had flown in from other states with their families for Christmas and the normal chaos ensued with kids and extra people. Kim reports that there were no overt hostile words or behavior; the surface was quiet. Even so, both daughters changed airline tickets, which were slapped with significant penalties, and left earlier than planned.

As Kim talked about her girls leaving she began to cry, "My children have never liked my second husband and vice-versa. Jerod is a know-it-all. He doesn't initiate conversation or indicate any interest in my kids' lives but butts in when they talk and makes snide comments and tells them what they should have done or should do in the future. He can't shut up. And after the fact if he's said something inappropriate and I point it out, he can't see it. He says I'm being a 'bitch.'

"Jerod also has a way of dead-ending conversations. He dogs us. When I want to have a private conversation with the girls that have nothing to do with him, there he is. He insinuates himself into every conversation and even follows us into the bedroom.

"I could see my daughters becoming upset so I talked to Jerod and explained nicely that I have few opportunities to be with them, would he please cut us some slack. He was insulted. He said, 'What did I do? I just want to be part of the family.'

"Jerod does not have a clue that his behavior is a problem or pretends he doesn't have a clue, I don't know which because he is very intelligent. He sits around taking everything in, and then jumps in with nasty words and acts innocent or he leaves. Everyone is chatting and suddenly he stands up and leaves the room.

"I can manage him for the most part when we're alone but that's really what I do—manage him."

I asked Kim what she meant 'manage him.'

Kim responded, "For two weeks, sometimes three weeks, he's quiet and into himself, although he makes cranky comments regularly, probably daily. I'm so used to his talk I don't even hear it. At least that's what my girls say.

"Then out of the blue he starts. If I ask him to do something around the house, he says that if I weren't such a rotten housekeeper he wouldn't have to be put to so much trouble. I usually ignore his words because they are just silly; the truth is we have an immaculate house. Then he says my spending is out of control, which is ridiculous because compared to him I'm a miser. And, really, I am a miser. I can't even stand to buy clothes for myself unless I'm forced into it. We have plenty of money. Jerod makes huge bonuses every year. We have company stock and other stock.

"In other words he just says and does anything that pops into his mind. He can be very nice but when he's upset about something, mainly because it's not his idea, he becomes a verbal maniac. He'll suddenly leave the house without saying anything, go to the store and come back with stuff we don't need.

"Jerod never acknowledges that what he has said or done is wrong and definitely never agrees that his behavior is inappropriate, but then he is quiet and contrite for a few days. I've always accepted his behavior, thinking that's the way he is.

"Now with my kids unwilling to put up with him, I really feel torn and want to do something about my situation. What should I do?"

Good question. "What do you want to do?"

Kim was blank, "I'm not sure."

**POSSIBLE SOLUTIONS:** Kim and Jerod's coupling is passive, impulsive and aggressive. Evidently the two of them know their parts and without interruption their passive, impulsive and aggressive roles continue unabated regardless of the observation of houseguests.

To interrupt this perfect fit will be difficult unless Kim is dedicated to change and able to follow through. From her story it sounds like either she is seeking therapy because she is able to see herself through her daughters' eyes or it may be she called for counseling to appease her daughters, to let them know she is doing something.

For herself, she "manages."

**QUESTIONABLE SOLUTIONS:** Unless Jerod experiences his behavior as dystonic there is no reason for him to change. His behavior relieves his tension and an added bonus is power over Kim.

Kim's commitment to therapy and positive change will make or break the marriage because therapy will be a threat to Jerod. He prefers the status quo and he will definitely work to make sure Kim gives up treatment.

So, we will see.


## BE IMPULSIVE AND LOSE THE HIGH GROUND

As an impulsive person you think quickly and act quickly. A thought comes to mind and you immediately say or act out the thought. The problem is, anxiety is only temporarily relieved and your relationship has taken another hit.

When you impulsively react then, "Oops, sorry, I didn't mean to say that," won't fly indefinitely. Or you may not be sorry. You gain pleasure from acting impulsively—sometimes with a mean spirit.

Tension makes it difficult to get beyond your experience and be empathic. You are flooded with overwhelming, powerful thoughts that must be put into action. You have a reputation; everyone knows how you are. Words just bubble up and out. What can you do? You are the victim of your mind.

Au contraire, your actions and reactions are voluntary. The after effect to the relationship for saying or doing whatever comes to mind is trouble. Because a thought came to mind does not mean it has merit.

Anxiety, based in fear, underlies your impulsive thought processes. To capture your own attention and take charge of impulsive behavior increases anxiety so it is difficult to stop and think, "Gee, these thoughts and their consequent behavior don't work. I think I will stop this."

The impulsive action pays off momentarily as your tension decreases and you feel powerful. The powerful feeling does not last long since the next step is defending your position to a partner who is angry and has backed away.

These are questions to determine whether or not you are impulsive:

1. Do quick reactions express real thoughts and feelings?
2. Do you have to back pedal or apologize after you act?
3. Do you **have to** say what you are thinking or you cannot stand the tension.
4. Are you are so caught up in your need to speak that your partner's point of view disappears.

The ability to look into the self is not a God-given right. Few people are blessed with self insight. However, you do know if you are getting what you want in your relationship and whether you are pleased with your actions and communication style.

A conscious program meant to take charge of the self is required for change and that can be daunting *but you can do it*. Change is in yourself interest. Each night for at least one week record how you controlled impulses that day. In fact, continue to note daily control as well as positive experiences since studies have shown that recording at least three positive experiences before bed elevates both intellectual and emotional happiness.

## RIGID DEFENSES DO NOT HAPPINESS BRING

These three defensive positions, impulsive, passive and passive aggressive, are habit-driven and difficult to "see" - as in seeing and understanding how we are in the world. The paradox of attention to thoughts and thereby focusing on developing desirable conscious thought processes is that as thoughts become automatic, the ability to see and hear the thought disappears. The defensive stance has dropped into the unconscious as a habit that does not require conscious focus.

Even though our defenses may not work in our best interests, like drug addicts we cling to our defensive avoidance positions as if defenses are lifeboats and we are drowning. The holes in the defensive lifeboat can be patched, we can ditch the boat and find new ways to paddle and sail through life or, of course, we can go down with the ship.

Take heart! Be courageous! Speak non-defensively—strip off that coat of fear and be yourself.

Defensive avoidance is one explanation for why you just aren't happy. Another explanation is detailed in Section Three, The Communication Pit. Negative habits of mind generated by our family of origin, genetic programming or low self-esteem are projected on others through the language of our relationships resulting in communication that disrupts instead of connecting partners.

# SECTION THREE

## GOOD COMMUNICATION

Good communication can be defined easily:

1. You express your thoughts clearly and try to understand what the other person is saying.
2. You express feelings openly and directly and encourage the other person to do the same.

Communication is a barometer of relationship status. Positive words, tone and body language flow when you feel happy. Conversely, troubled talk is argumentative and contradictory, indicating a lack of interest in or rejection of another person's feelings, actions or point of view.

Negative emotions are aroused when communication is riddled with complaints, criticism, sarcasm, and contempt or withholding. This generates agitation, frustration and disrespect. A free and smooth flowing interaction is no longer possible because neither party can relax for fear that a casual remark will suddenly turn into a negative experience. Chapters Eleven and Twelve demonstrate negative communication.

## CHAPTER ELEVEN

# I'M JUST NOT HAPPY...DIFFICULT COMMUNICATION: COMPLAINTS AND CRITICISM

## TROUBLED TALK

Your partner refuses to listen to you or share his or her feelings. He is argumentative or defensive, insisting that his thoughts and feelings are all that count. Ultimatums, a loud, hissing voice, dismissing and diminishing your thoughts with criticism or sarcasm get his message across by inflaming or dead ending communication.

Or, rather than being direct, he may communicate by passively acting out his feelings. He is silent or shows displeasure with facial expressions and body movements, (shrugging shoulders, rolling eyes, dismissive hand movements), and then acts innocent when asked what that means.

You are familiar with body talk. Even a stranger's face portrays basic, universal emotional codes recognized across all cultures. Sadness, anger, fear, disgust, embarrassment, joy or happiness present an emotional book anyone can open.

In an intimate relationship your partner not only opens the book, he reads it. Your face, tone and body language present your partner with an emotional map and under the best circumstances that map leads to empathy and understanding. When, instead of understanding, body talk is used to convey displeasure without subsequent clarifying discussion, confusion reigns.

Confusion is the operative word to describe Frances and Roger's relationship. Decoding their verbal and physical messages was next to impossible.

## BARBED WIRE BARRIERS

Frances and Roger called for marriage counseling when they finally acknowledged that talking together and being happy were an oxymoron. Critical words had a way of creeping into every conversation.

## FRANCES AND ROGER: HOW TO TALK YOURSELF INTO UNHAPPINESS

A simple conversation between Frances & Roger turns into an emotionally disturbing experience where the intent of communication, connecting, is lost. Instead, words are used to baffle, express disdain or as a call to combat.

Frances and Roger live together on the emotional edge. They cannot wait for a chance to express contemptuous words couched in innocent sounding bewilderment. Volatile at a moment's notice, feelings simmer, waiting for the right look, the right twitch or the right word, then a mix of criticism and sarcasm explodes like a bomb.

## THERAPY

Frances and Roger walked into their first marriage counseling session holding hands. They agree that their most troubling problems are daily arguments and fighting with occasional physical bouts (and that is about the last time they agreed).

In their first therapy session Frances gazes into Roger's eyes, pauses, then poses a question to me. She wants to know who is right. "I have an example for you.

Saturday mornings I go to college, Roger goes to work at 11, but he takes care of my four-year-old Melanie until her father, Brad, appears.

"Last Saturday Roger told me he called Brad at 11:10. Brad hadn't shown up and Roger was agitated and, I suppose, worried about getting to work. Brad told him to "----" off, that he'd get there when he was good and ready. Roger exploded and Brad hung up on him.

"I got home from school a few minutes later and I totally agreed with what Roger told Brad. I was enraged. I called Brad and began to chew him out BUT Roger told me to calm down. 'Not in front of Mel,' he said. I agreed and when Brad finally came to pick up Mel I told him that he, Roger and I needed to talk. 'Let's have a phone conference Monday.' He grunted in agreement.

"Roger left for work and I thought everything was cool. Then came the bomb and this is what always happens. Roger called from his car phone and began quietly talking about Brad's behavior. He said he was shocked that I hadn't stood up for him. He was disgusted with me. If the situation had been reversed he would not have put up with it."

With a dramatic roll of her eyes—a behavior sure to be seen as a put down—Frances feigned surprise and innocence: "He's criticizing me. I was dumbfounded. I was really p....d so I said, 'You are the one who suggested I not talk to Brad in front of Mel. I tried to take your side and you cut me off!' He ignored this so I lost it, I went crazy on him.

"We are constantly in this state where I think we are on the same track doing what Roger wants when wham! He slams me." Frances's shrill tone was escalating.

Roger wasn't going to take that lying down. He interrupted with, "My whole damn job on the weekends is to keep Frances calm, Saturday was no exception. When I left that morning I could tell she was seething so I called her from my car just to make sure she was OK." He trailed off as if he was so disgusted with her rendition of reality that it was useless to even talk about it.

How did this couple come to vie for the status of "I am the real victim, the person who is slighted and misunderstood?"

## WORD POWER

Roger, 33, is soft-spoken and personable with very definite ideas about everything from child-rearing to what should be on National Public Radio. Fit and tan, an ex-hockey coach, now a wholesale wine sales rep, Roger has happily taken the role of dad for Fran's three kids, ages 4 to 16. His child rearing/husband orientation, dad as head of the household and boss, is like honey to a bee. Frances loves the idea of Roger as the family's protector. She just cannot agree with his family-man style.

Frances, 37, is Roger's counterpart. Where he smiles, fits in, quietly moves around, Fran is an in-your-face live wire whose unusual appearance matches her personality. Her features and coloring don't quite fit together, blue eyes, light hair, olive skin, skewed by an unusually large mouth and teeth. Fran's large mouth fits her personality; she is argumentative and boisterous.

Roger lays the groundwork for trouble by quietly making an provocative statement, "I see that the kids are falling behind in their chores, probably because they aren't being supervised like we agreed."

Gazing at her with what appears to be love and tenderness, he's sorry she's so "thin-skinned." Then he begins to defend and explain himself, pointing out that she is wrong, and his feelings are hurt by her words.

Because of his calm, quiet and definitive presentation Frances cannot figure out that Roger is a critical person. She flies at his words and then she becomes the scapegoat, hysterical and mean, the person who started the fight.

Whose interpretation of reality is the real truth?

## THE PRIMITIVE ADULT

In marriage and in life our job is growth and development, which means maturing and learning from experience.

Instead of maturing, Frances and Roger are boxed in; they frighten one another. They act out their deepest, most primitive fear by casting fear's shadow on their partner. In psychological parlance, that's called projection.

Frances feels criticized and Roger feels misunderstood; they each feel abandoned, alone and unprotected. Consequently, critical words slice at the core of their beings, coloring and distorting what they hear. They cling to one another like abused children at the same time that they lash out, screaming contemptuous words with an occasional respite of "love" to forge their primitive bond.

## THERAPY

The immediate focus of therapy was to stop the word battle. Roger and Frances seem to experience perverse pleasure in dramatically expressing anger and then being huffy about the other person's mirroring behavior. Getting these two to settle down and listen rather than focus on what was going on in their head (confused, crazed, critical dialogue) was a daunting task because each did a U-turn back to, "I'm not wrong".

**IMMEDIATE PROBLEM:** Communication equals confusion.

**IMMEDIATE SOLUTION:** Stop yourself before you utter a negative word or phrase—even in mid-phrase. If your partner tells you that your words are negative or hurtful, at that moment acknowledge that that is what your partner thinks and feels. Do not dispute or argue! Expect your mind to throw up argumentative and defensive thoughts. Do not verbalize those thoughts.

When your partner speaks do not immediately respond. Take a few seconds to sooth and calm yourself. Then preface any communication with, "I understand you think…." after which you present your version of what you have just heard in a soft voice. If you are confused, say so, stay calm and listen until you understand. If you are unable to remain calm, you are the problem, not your spouse.

**LONG TERM PROBLEM:** Both Frances and Roger have self-esteem issues and lack interpersonal communication skills.

**LONG TERM SOLUTION:** Calm and untangle communication experiences and set up boundaries. Boundaries: This is what I feel and think; you are allowed to think and feel differently.

Both individual and conjoint therapy are necessary to stop the verbal bloodletting. Psychotherapy will alter skewed personal perspectives and conjoint therapy will provide learning tools to appreciate and work with, not against, their partner. But, can these two personalities sit still long enough to think differently and alter their communication? Time will tell.

## COMMUNICATION STYLE

Like Frances and Roger, we all have personal communication styles wrapped around our defense systems. Although others recognize our distinctive styles we have an unconscious, defensive brain grid that allows us to be in the dark about our own behavior.

If you are a "muller" you take time to come to conclusions, to react, to decide just how you feel and what you think. Impulsive speakers talk first and think later. They blurt out their opinions and let the chips fall.

Within the range of mulling over and speaking impulsively are communication patterns that soothe and smooth relationship paths and others that confound and confuse with complaints, criticism, sarcasm or the defensive wall of silence. These confounding patterns result in distress if you are the recipient; the temptation is to insist that your partner stop criticizing, condemning or complaining, which works as well as hitting yourself on the head with a hammer. If, on the other hand, your partner's pattern is to stop communicating then you may insist he talk, which doesn't work either.

When your responses do not change your partner's patterns the first 20 times, then guess what? Either he is choosing to play deaf or his unconscious brain grid will not allow a docking neuron. Either way your words fall on deaf ears.

And, we are back to the idea that you are right, your partner wrong and your happiness depends on your partner, "If only he would stop criticizing" or "If he would just talk to me and tell me what's on his mind," in effect, telling yourself that you are not in charge.

Is it you or is it him?

## PROBLEMS AND SOLUTIONS

Because we are social animals we need to talk. Our happiness, moods, and capacity to flourish are enormously influenced by interactions with others as well as self dialogue. When your partner refuses to speak or if dialogue is laced with complaints, criticism or sarcasm, communication is dead-ended.

## CHECK OUT YOUR COMMUNICATION PATTERN

Words as well as behavior constitute communication. The following are dead-end patterns. Do you:

1. Deliberately push buttons—poke at your partner's vulnerable areas.

2. Act innocent, stare blankly or say nothing when you know what's going on.
3. Divert attention.
4. Downplay his emotions.
5. Act emotionless and flat-lined.

If you see yourself participating in any of the above behaviors, do not excuse yourself to yourself. Instead, acknowledge and alter your bad behavior. Your words and behavior are a defense of pretense; you know you are dead-ending communication and your partner knows it.

## SHORT-CIRCUITING COMMUNICATION

These communication dead enders are muddy, indirect discussion closures and generally fly under the radar of criticism but each method either borders on criticism or presents flat out disapproval.

1. Right: Knows the answer, disregards your point of view.
2. Defensive: Cannot take responsibility for his actions. You are wrong.
3. Expert: Solves your problem whether you want him to or not.
4. Silent: Because you disagree she will not talk.
5. Martyr: Immediately and dramatically becomes the victim.
6. Stoic: Responds to feelings with disdain.
7. Harps: Constant complaints or criticisms.
8. History Buff: Brings up every past hurt.

Once you recognize your partner's style you have an opportunity to respond differently, not by pointing out his or her communication shortcomings, but by altering your thinking.

## HOW TO THINK ABOUT AND HANDLE CRITICISM

The critic's communication habit can include a quick, in passing, put down or a disturbing, incessant commentary about you, his imperfect partner. Jackie and Doug are an example of criticism that has gained momentum through the years and is the hallmark of their relationship.

## THE CRITICS: JACKIE AND DOUG

Through their 12 years together Jackie and Doug have gradually picked up their critical pace with one another until life is a battleground.

Doug, 36, is a sales rep, casually well dressed, a quick-thinking talker, used to getting his way, who needs cleanliness and order at home. Jackie, 34, is an occasional dress designer, but more often at home with two preschool children. She is slender, very pretty with curly black hair, blue eyes and a lot to say, particularly about her perceived shortcomings.

In their first therapy session together Jackie begins by putting herself down, "I know my own faults, at least," with a significant glance at Doug, "I'm scatterbrained. I go from one thing to another without finishing anything. Some days I clean and some days I don't. I yell at the kids incessantly one day, the next I'm patient. This drives Doug up the wall. I hate the end of the day when he comes home because I know he's going to walk in, point out something I didn't do and be mad. He's very critical of me." Jackie is fighting back tears.

Doug had been staring at Jackie during her discourse as though he was slightly amused but puzzled by her talk. "Of course I'm disturbed when I get home and the house is the same mess it was the day before and the kids are skidding around the house yelling. It's chaos.

"Frankly, I think Jackie is depressed and needs medication. She is scattered. She's never been able to figure out how to clean the house. Such a simple thing." Looking at me for confirmation, "Anyone can clean a house. House cleaners are paid minimum wage and, yet, Jackie is confounded by any household task. She's not stupid."

"Well," Jackie interrupted, "I don't criticize you daily." Doug interjected, "No, every other day." Jackie continued, crying and blowing her nose, "It wears a person down. He wants to control me. This is what happens all the time. He's mad. I'm upset. He criticizes me and then won't talk to me. I'm upset and then I get angry and say things I shouldn't and Doug retaliates. We go around and around. I just don't think I can take it anymore. I want out."

Doug's reply, "I do not want a divorce. I love Jackie and I want the marriage." When he said that Jackie instantly switched her position, said she loved him too but doesn't want to be upset constantly.

## WHERE DOES THE BUCK STOP?

Who is going to take charge, be the bigger person, and stop criticizing? There are couples who need to bicker, argue and destroy good feelings. They may be masochists, they may be control freaks, they may be obsessive and they may repress the disturbance and consequently have no motivation to change.

Jackie and Doug state vehemently that they hate their communication style, yet their critical tit for tat has continued, unabated, for 12 years. To arrive at a juncture of agreed-upon positive action is a dramatic alteration in their relationship.

**SHORT AND LONG TERM SOLUTION:** Here is how each is to take charge of critical thoughts and behavioral habits:

1. I am responsible for my words.
2. I acknowledge that I have been critical and I am sorry.

3. I choose not to speak critically.
4. I need help. If you hear critical words, please tell me.
5. Tell me in writing.
6. I am happy to have you help me. I want you to help me.

Pointing out critical words to one another may seem like throwing a hand grenade and not expecting an explosion, but the trick here is learning to listen and acknowledge the other person's words and emotions.

Jackie and Doug's immediate, defensive historical response would have been to slap back with criticism. Instead, deliberate control is exerted while words are processed and the brain is allowed time to register change.

## CRITICAL LABELS

Unhappy relationships follow a pattern. Eventually a pattern of critical words establishes labels that in turn develop a grid in the mind. Critical labels include, "You are… slow, dumb, mean, selfish, poor housekeeper, poor provider," etc.

Doug labels Jackie scatterbrained, impulsive, and angry. Jackie labels Doug critical, mean, and controlling. Habitual thoughts easily reinforce the label. Doug thinks, 'She jumps from one thing to another, can't even keep the house clean." Jackie thinks, 'He views me as stupid and incompetent. How mean."

We establish labels in our mind to enable us to think faster. Labels set up a grid where words and behavior dock without thought. For example, Doug might say, "She has a lot on her mind," meaning she is forgetful with good reason, but if, instead, he calls her scatterbrained, indicating she is incapable of straight thinking, the label defines her mind as deficient and automatically drops into Doug's pre-set silent grid—stupid (even though he verbalizes that she is smart). The grid is sticky, labels are not easily shaken and each negative thought reinforces the label while it drives the relationship deeper into dislike and distrust.

Jackie and Doug continued therapy for two years to sort out their individual and couple bad habits. Communication was their focus. Because they were dedicated and actively seeking change, each person dramatically altered thinking patterns and found a middle road of happiness.

## FOCUS ON THE SELF

Dedication to your own transformation can and will absolutely alter your relationship—you can change your life dramatically all by yourself.

First, examine your interactions. If there is any possibility that you are critical, either by your own or your partner's assessment, clear your own slate first.

You say," What about him? He should stop saying upsetting things to me." Yes, he should. We will figure out how to handle his critical style in the next few pages but, are you going to wait for him to change, or will you take command of yourself?

Do you:

1. Criticize
2. Complain
3. Irritate easily
4. Overreact/attack
5. Jump to conclusions
6. Exaggerate or minimize
7. Act depressed and moody
8. Act defensive if he suggests he is displeased
9. Educate (you know best and definitively communicate your knowledge)

Or, your communication style may be helpful:

1. Patient
2. Good listener
3. Loving
4. Solution-oriented
5. Insight-oriented
6. Accommodating
7. Kind and generous

Pay attention to your reactions. In fact, write down your thoughts in response to your partner's words for a week and you will discover a very interesting life form. Your brain has patterned communication maps.

When you have concrete information about your habitual pattern of reacting instead of blurry, defensive, "I didn't mean that, I didn't say that, I am right", you have ammunition for yourself, something specific to work on.

Congratulate yourself for positive behaviors and then choose a critical behavior that you want to alter or eliminate. Write it down on several cards. Put one on your home mirror, one on the dashboard of your car, one on your desk and one on your kitchen counter. Write the behavior in shorthand so that your personal life is not public.

It is important that you are not nagged about change, "Oh, so you are going to change. Right!" Before you make any announcement about your personal dedication to change make sure others will be helpful, otherwise you sabotage yourself.

John Gottman, Ph.D., who has spent 30 years researching marriage satisfaction, has found that if one or both partners' communication is filled with the need to criticize and condemn, the marriage is on a slippery downward slope. Gottman also found that stonewalling, presenting a stone wall, i.e., silence, choosing not to respond, shutting down and turning away, is another stepping-stone to unhappiness and relationship dissolution.

## ALTERING YOUR RESPONSE IN THE FACE OF CRITICISM

To alter the habit of either arguing or folding when you are criticized rather than standing up for yourself effectively sounds easy, but if you have put up with criticism, it may be very difficult to talk to your partner with ease. Your reaction has probably been pitifully defensive or ineffectively aggressive.

Mentally practice what you will say in the face of critical words. Practice simple phrases over and over until they are second nature and then speak directly the moment you hear a critical remark. For example, "I realize you may not mean to criticize me," or "You may not be aware that those words are critical but they hurt my feelings."

And if your partner replies, "So what?" or "You are too sensitive", or "You are misinterpreting my words," stand your ground. Do not cave. Your partner is dodging, being defensive or is downright aggressive and mean. Stay clear-headed. Do not argue. You are stating a fact and if your words are thrown back at you, the discussion is over.

Immediately go to your computer or journal and jot down exactly what has been said while your memory is clear. Fear and anticipatory anxiety or argumentative defensiveness keeps you spinning, caught in the same emotional quagmire. A transcript reveals facts.

The point is to shine a spotlight on reality so that you calm down, think clearly, react only to facts and establish a plan of conscious, effective word action.

## CONSCIOUS WORDS & ACTS

Once words are spoken they cannot be taken back. You can think anything and dismiss the thought but the spoken word goes into your mind and may never leave. Mean-spirited words, criticism and constant complaining or the negative experience of disrespect, contempt or silence are chilling intimacy breakers.

The habit of complaining is different than criticism. Criticism is blame, distorting character and globally undermining a person's personality. Complaints are specific to a person, place or thing. An occasional relationship complaint is expected but habitual complaints do not invite a flow of ideas or even a reply.

## RACHEL: THE WHINER

Even therapists get tired of a complainer. It is one thing to verbalize unhappiness and look for a solution but Rachel, 36 years old, has spent her life whining and miserable about the past and the present, and of course, continues to complain in therapy.

Rachel presents herself as unable to change any thought process and in her first therapy session says, "Why am I always unhappy? I love my house but I don't want to do anything in my house. I'm always negative with Hank (her live-in friend). I don't want to touch him or really have anything to do with him even though Hank does everything for me. He cleans the house; he makes dinner and he's generous but I'm just not happy."

I asked Rachel when she started feeling this way and she said, "I'm not sure, I think since we bought the house. I know when we were going together I thought Hank was nice-looking and nice to me. We hardly ever had sex then because he had a problem but he's had a penile implant since then. He really just did it for me.

"Even so, I don't want to have sex with him. Isn't that awful? I went with Tony for four years and we had sex all the time. I couldn't wait to get my hands on him but with Hank, I'm not interested. I say mean things to him, too. I don't know why."

Rachel sounds like a complaining, whiney baby who has no choices in life. Everything and everybody has been thrust upon her. She has been feeling unhappy and complaining for years. Hank is the first relationship she has had with a nice man, she says. All other men in her life ran around with other women or were married— except her first husband who she fought with all the time. He was mean and verbally abusive. Still, Rachel tells me, "I wish I hadn't divorced my first husband. I keep thinking that and I even tell Hank that. Then I wouldn't have to work."

The present is not reality. Rachel lives in past misery and clings to her unhappiness as a badge of honor. She has no choice; she wallows in pity and continually says, "Why do I do that?" Meaning, why do I keep thinking these thoughts?

And when I say, "Yes. Why do you continuously think those thoughts?" Rachel smirks and then I know we are doing a one-eighty back to where we started.

Rachel, like a ping pong ball, calls for therapy every couple of years which tells me she is interested in change (or interested in complaining to someone besides Hank) but has not grown enough to grasp that she is responsible for her thoughts and, therefore, her life.

## COMPLAINT AS A LIFE STYLE

Rachel harps, scolds and continuously complains. She has a defensive complaint style that keeps others away while she pleasantly wallows in her unhappiness.

If you live with a person like Rachel you need survival techniques.

**SURVIVAL:** Living with a complainer requires bold, business-like techniques:

1.    Write down the words of complaint exactly.

2.  Ask yourself, "Do the words have validity?"
3.  Reacting to a complaining partner with anger, sullen behavior or withdrawal is not effective.
4.  Neutralize your thoughts about the complaints before you discuss the words. You want to be objective and learn what is going on in your partner's mind (maybe nothing).
5.  Tell your partner you want to sit down at a convenient time and talk. Let her decide when and where but do not let the matter drop. If she does not suggest a time, you set the time.
6.  When you discuss complaints begin by reading your partner's exact words. Do not editorialize.
7.  Do not allow her to add other subjects or move away from the point you are making.
8.  Your job is to find out what your spouse is thinking. You need information.
9.  If the words reflect a problem she has with you and she can talk seriously about what she has said, take her seriously and look at yourself.
10. If her words are simply mean-spirited and meant to hurt, the next time a complaint is aimed at you, you understand the mind it came from, you do not jump for the bait and get pulled into the complaint vortex.

Whatever the outcome you are putting your spouse on notice that you will no longer simply react to her words, instead, you will have a talk. And, with this information you have an opportunity to alter your interactions and, thereby, either make changes or accept that forevermore you are chained to an unhappy, dissatisfied person.

The next chapter focuses on how to handle the issue of contempt, sarcasm or the refusal to speak.

## CHAPTER TWELVE

# I'M JUST NOT HAPPY...MY PARTNER EITHER WON'T SPEAK, IS SARCASTIC, OR TREATS ME WITH CONTEMPT

### CONTEMPT AND SARCASM

Contempt is scorn. Scorn evaluates another as unworthy and dismisses him or her as a person of value. Sarcasm is an accelerated and virulent form of criticism. Both complaints and criticism are direct dislikes of something specific whereas contempt and sarcasm slide into your mind with clever, indirect words often accompanied by subtle facial nuances that indicate you are discounted and stupid.

You know you have been slimed, and you immediately feel the message but interpretation may take a minute. "That was smart." "It's too bad you couldn't have thought of that yourself."

If you protest and indicate you are upset by the implication, tone or words, you will be met by a response that indicates that you are:

1.   Too sensitive,
2.   Lacking in understanding,
3.   Taking everything too seriously.,
4.   Minus a sense of humor,
5.   Making your partner mad by your response; or
6.   Unable to communicate.

A person who resorts to sarcasm is a word bully who is uninterested in your protestations, rather, he enjoys his sarcastic style and views himself as clever and in command.

Sarcasm with children is an abuse of power; sarcasm with adults is a form of verbal abuse. The intent of sarcasm is to raise yourself in your own eyes and diminish the other person, and is meant to harm and injure the other person's character.

Sarcasm takes place in private and public. In public sarcasm has a quality of humiliation and embarrassment. If those present are silent, the implication is tacit approval and, therefore, a confirmation of the abuse.

In private, sarcasm is frequently constant and dedicated. The person who is abused may seem only dimly aware and even deny that he or she is being verbally abused.

## JUDITH: SARCASM

In her first therapy session Judith stated that her family was her problem: "If I call my kids, who are grown, they talk to me for about two minutes max, seldom accept any invitation to visit and, this really hurts me, none of them invite me over."

In a later session Judith acknowledged that she is occasionally sarcastic. Her sarcasm is "funny" and Judith reports, "They know I'm just joking."

No, they do not know you are joking. The implication is that if they take your words seriously, they are in error. This is a typical response that claims innocence while refusing responsibility for hurting others.

## THE DISCONNECT

Little makeup, basic hair with enough curls to know she had a perm somewhere along the way, Judith is a solid, big-boned woman. She wears snappy, expensive tailored clothes and then completes her ensemble with scuffed shoes.

Judith, 43, knows who she is in the business world. She's powerful, third in command in a large insurance company where she states that she can make decisions and solve any problem with a sense of humor, but when discussions veer into the personal, emotional realm, clear thinking disappears. Judith jumps under a sarcastic cover.

Strangely enough, a disconnect occurs between others' sarcastic comments which "destroy" her and Judith's view of her own nasty, "light-hearted" responses. When her family retorts by disappearing or engaging in tit–for–tat talk Judith feels bitter, indignant and offended but does not grasp the fact that she is a major player in these interactions.

## MEAN PARENTS BEGET MEAN PARENTS

Sarcasm that sounds confident, bold and aggressive is fear-based. Judith learned in her family of origin to be highly sensitive to her own emotions and at the same time to ignore the feelings of others.

Judith is devastated by hurtful comments just as she was when her critical, authoritarian mother screeched and raged, "Get out of my sight. You make me sick," "What's wrong with you?" And more directly, "I'm sorry I ever had a child like you."

When Judith was in seventh grade she was honored for her artistic ability at a school banquet. Her mother told her after she accepted the award, "Couldn't you have thought of something better to say?" and said Judith walked up to accept the award like a "cripple." These contemptuous parental words and behaviors swirled together, baked Judith's feelings and informed the relationship portion of her thought processes to be on guard and ready either to be the attacker or the attackee.

As an adult Judith no longer needs to protect herself and ward off the blows and arrows of childhood but the habit of sarcasm lives on, invisible to her. She is miserable and cannot grasp why the family is mean to her.

Judith has failed in her development to launch past the need to protect her ego.

**IMMEDIATE PROBLEM:** The first issue is to recognize and acknowledge an habitual, sarcastic style and secondly, to spell out specifics: When, where and with whom are you sarcastic.

1. When you are told your words hurt, whether you believe they should or should not, accept that others have a right to their experience. Acknowledge their feelings.
2. The minute you realize you have spoken sarcastically, apologize. Whether the realization comes seconds after you have spoken or two days later, acknowledge to yourself and to the other person that you were inappropriate.
3. Catalogue situations, particular people and how or why you react sarcastically. Visual written proof provides facts that cannot be swept away.

Decide exactly how to attack your habit.

Sarcasm is mean-spirited and has negative consequences, but since sarcastic thoughts naturally come to mind, eliminating the sarcastic slice-and-dice mode is difficult. Be prepared for resistance from yourself as there is powerful pleasure in the sarcastic sucker-punch feeling of control.

Also, be prepared to be tenacious. Managing those thoughts requires an unnatural amount of attention to your mind processes. You will need to:

1. Use your business mind to change course.
2. Rehearse positive responses.

3. Keep your goal in mind—eliminate sarcastic responses.
4. Stay conscious. That means the minute you resort to old unconscious habits, old words will surface.
5. As an executive you order others to make alterations. Order your own alterations and stick with the alteration.

Desire and motivation determine results.

## LONG TERM SOLUTION: The Brave Solution

1. Tell family members your plan. Tell them that you are aware of your communication style and are actively working on change.
2. They can be helpful to you by pointing out sarcastic comments only if you prepare yourself for their comments and are thankful.
3. The minute you experience hurt or anger, settle down, take a deep breath and remember your goal.
4. This is a long-term project, patience is required.
5. You are not trying to change anyone else so skip any "What about you?" talk.

In therapy Judith's sarcastic style received a psychological chelation. Chelation exchanges sick bodily fluids for healthy blood; Judith is exchanging old, poisonous thoughts for healthy, new ideas and understandings. Just like a marrow transplant, the diseased experience is examined, extricated and replaced.

Talking about change is simple; putting new ideas into effect can be hard. Judith is continually working with herself, controlling her words and trying to overcome hurt feelings as she turns herself into a nice person and receives intentional and unintentional pay back. Judith's family is warming up but not quite welcoming her with open arms since they do not trust her recovery from a sarcastic mind set—yet.

## MESSAGES FROM THE PAST

Looking at other's relationships with parents is informative but never as informative as looking at your own relationship history with its unusual twists and turns. Briefly let yourself think about the past. What messages did you receive? Quickly jot down the first thought that comes to mind about your parents' relationship, the first thought about how your mother talked to your father, the first thought about how your father talked your mother. How did each communicate with you?

1.

2.

3.

4.

Do you experience any of these behaviors in your marriage? If so, does it make you feel good? Does it enhance your marriage?

Sometimes you know you sound like one of your parents but cannot quite get the words changed—or you may not want to. If your partner comments by pointing out, "You sound like your mother/father," the comment feels derogatory.

Those words can help you look at yourself but only if you are able to do two things: avoid defensiveness and de-personalize. De-personalize means you step back and can objectively analyze what was said rather than go into your baby self of hurt feelings. If you are sarcastic you literally slap back, "How dare you! O.K. Let's talk about *your* mother!"

If you drop the defensiveness and de-personalize you have a chance to think objectively about what has been said, decide if the words do or do not have merit and, most importantly, ask your partner, "In what way am I talking like my mother?" The question to your partner is two-edged. You are taking your partner seriously and checking to see if the words have merit or were mean-spirited.

And even if you are hyperventilating and filled with anxiety or anger after your partner's comments, remember you are grown up and have control of yourself. You can cool down and think.

As the recipient of sarcasm fear has been drilled into you; you anticipate words and behavior that hurt and cut to the bone. The defenses meant to protect you actually make you feel powerless and pitiful.

But, you are only as powerless as you allow yourself to be; you have the ability to change reactions. Here's how.

## HOW TO CHANGE THINKING STYLES

Neuroscientists have confirmed that attention exerts real, physical effects on the brain. In other words, if you want to change any habit, mental effort and steady attention to the desired change will alter your brain's neuroplasticity, where 10,000 new brain cells are manufactured every day. When you are serious, steady and focused on what you want, your brain will react to those thoughts and just like a drill sergeant giving orders, brain cells salute, rewire and forge new connections

You are in charge of your brain. Give your brain orders. Demand energy or concentration this minute. You are talking to yourself all of the time. The trick is: Do not let your interior whiner or critical brain take over and automatically react, "Why would he say that and hurt my feelings?" "Oh, I'm so tired. I can't do that right now, maybe later." Or, "So I said a few mean things, everyone does, and, (to yourself), 'they deserve it'." No thought is required for these reactions, they are old, tired and, if you think about them, dumb.

Just as muscles can be built, thinking patterns can be changed—with your active attention. Attention means that, "I am aware of what I am doing while I am doing it, aware of what I am thinking, aware of the words I speak and most of all aware of my goal. I am in the here and now." The reward for your attention and action: self-satisfaction and happiness.

Just as the noise of inner or outer words is a form of communication so is the deafening sound of silence.

## THE SOUND OF SILENCE

Deliberate silence is a form of communication called withholding. Without words you can guess what your partner is thinking, often an educated guess but, still, unless he tells you, you are in the dark. If he feels so strongly that he is struck dumb and cannot speak after the fact of a disturbance, taking time to think about and then talk about a solution should be the conclusion. No.

He stays in control by never discussing the matter because, who knows, you may have a valid, different point of view and he does not want to hear it.

Living with a partner who goes for days without talking is like living with a bomb that is about to explode. Realistically and intellectually you might view his behavior as childish but isn't it weird that his silence puts you into a tense, anxious or angry state? Even though you know that he will not speak about his anger when he decides whatever has shut him down is over, still, you experience tension and live in your mind with the knowledge that the problem cannot be talked out and so, forever more, you partner on without a common solution and pretend everything is o.k.

Get a hold of yourself and take charge. Are you part of the problem? Do you over talk? Do you allow your partner to express himself? Do you insist on your version of reality so that negotiation is impossible? Do you put down any ideas he has?

Be honest with yourself and if any of these scenarios are true, when talk resumes mention your communication style, the difficulties he may have with your discussion methods and, if you are seriously altering your communication habits, point out that fact as well.

It is critical to understand that your partner chooses silence as a method to control the situation. The question is, what method will you use to resolve the fuming or anger or fear that is going on in your mind while you wait hours or days until the wall of silence slips away.

Here is what you do:

1. Stop dwelling on the silence.
2. Direct your mind to calm down.
3. Devise a plan.
4. You do not have to communicate. You feel uncomfortable with the silence. So what?
5. Go about your business. Silence is an opportunity to think your own thoughts.

Resolution comes through your mind set. You are living with a scared, silent person who is immobilized. It is important for you to stay off the fear train; you needn't be immobilized as well. Talk to yourself, write down positives and negatives about the situation, the issues and your partner's behavior.

For example:

| Positive | Negative |
|---|---|
| We do not fight. | We don't express emotions. |
| I like having alone time. | I feel lonely. |
| I am consciously serene. | I cannot stand silence. |
| I am thoughtful and focus on the relationship. | We are disengaged. |
| I prefer silence to anger. | I need to know why she is angry with me. |

By writing a good news and bad news list you qualify the here and now and stay away from running around like a rat in a maze with questions in your mind that do not have an answer. Let his need to shut you out remain his issue, not yours.

Knowledge is power. Once you firmly grasp the fact that silence is your partner's communication style you are in charge.

There are couples who find that talking together can be as much a problem as silence. Distressing, confusing talk is a shut off valve to connection and intimacy. There are brains that produce talk that disrupts, distracts, and circles back. Section Four describes talking disorders.

# SECTION FOUR

## TALKING DISORDERS

### THE COMMUNICATION PIT: DISTORTION, DISSOCIATION AND PERSONALIZATION

If your partner is in an accident and is brain-damaged your cry is not, "Why do you keep saying that?" or "Why do you do that when you know it upsets me?" You understand neurons in his brain have been compromised. But when distortion, dissociation or personalization are a part of your partner's communication style, you are unhappy, you know something is wrong with your interactions but putting your finger on the source is difficult and solving it seems impossible.

A talking disorder produces interactions that resemble trying to live in a house whose electrical wires go nowhere, short out and start fires. Conversations meander, confuse, frustrate, produce fruitless arguments and never have a beginning, middle or end point. How can you calmly discuss an issue and reach a conclusion when a firestorm is in process?

Like other skills, talking, listening and reaching a consensus take practice—the problem is that we think communication comes naturally. Unless you were born into a family of orators you honed communication skills by the seat of your pants. And, although invisible, the neurons in your brain or your spouse's brain that motor interactions, may be compromised.

Confusion, frustration and lack of intimacy are every-day issues when personalization, dissociation and distortion dominate communication and your relationship is in jeopardy because you or your partner feel:

1. Unloved
2. Can't talk without fighting
3. Sex life dull or null and void
4. On guard
5. Distrust
6. Problems unresolved
7. Lack of respect
8. Ignored

Each unresolved issue listed is a fissure that will crack marital rapport and connection. Once you recognize the source you can solve the problem. That means you will not be surprised or agitated by circular conversations and you will have the skills needed to listen and respond productively.

Chapters Thirteen, Fourteen and Fifteen describe distortion, dissociation and personalization.

## CHAPTER THIRTEEN

# DISTORTION

Distortion is a form of misinterpretation and phantom talk, some information is involved but you do not know what to make of it. A simple question begins a long response with irrelevant details but without an end point.

For example, you ask your wife a simple question, "Where were you?" She replies, "Well, Joan called about three o'clock and said she was going to Saks and wanted me to go along but I told her I had too much to do, so..." You wonder why she thinks that she is answering your question. You get frustrated and agitated by the long response (assuming you ever get to a response). If you show impatience or dissatisfaction, she may then get upset with you because first you ask a question and then don't want to listen to the answer.

The two of you now feel like ships passing in the night as you both head for the rocks. The result? Emotions are distorted.

Once the miscommunication takes hold, you'll both be all over the place: disappointed and shut down; angry one moment, conciliatory the next; or overly considerate or inconsiderate in a flash. Quickly you are sucked into a bewildering, elusive chaos where talking about issues or feelings compounds the problems; no solution or satisfaction is in the script.

So how do we correct this flawed communication? First, recognize that it is occurring.

## RECOGNIZING DISTORTIONS

Distortion is a misinterpretation of words or events. You say, "I'm going shopping with my sister Saturday." Your husband says, "You're always looking for ways to get away from me." This idea you ridicule because you've heard it before but, nevertheless, it puts you on guard.

If you take his words seriously and if you do go shopping, you must rush home or he will be upset because distortion engenders: guilt (your husband comes first, you are neglecting him), shame (you should not have a life of your own), or a struggle with control (he decides what you do).

On the other hand, you might understand his words as manipulation, truth or playfulness. Is he serious? Honestly—do you want to get away from him? Or, is he a funny guy? Does he shuck and jive? "You know I was kidding. You make everything a big deal." In other words he pretends he didn't mean anything and you are misinterpreting his words—maybe.

You understand that discussion is a distortion if:

1. You are puzzled and confused after a conversation.
2. Situations, words and feelings are out of proportion, either twisted, overly dramatic or made insignificant.
3. Terms like always, never, everyone, and nobody are used.
4. Experiences are good or bad, there is no grey area.

The distorter twists and turns conversations into a disturbing experience. Words meant to enlighten and connect snap rapport and inflame feelings.

## SIDESTEPPING: CATHY AND DEREK

Derek called for counseling because he said, "My wife, Cathy, and I have been married awhile and we seem to be sliding downhill. We have trouble talking without getting upset or into a fight. It's stupid because whatever we're talking about isn't that important."

Derek, 46, tall and lanky with a slightly forward tilt to his body, wears large, horn-rimmed glasses that give him an owl-like appearance. Derek informs me that he is a forensic psychologist and has come in alone for the first session to calm himself. Explaining his need for calm, "My wife turns everything around—situations, her feelings. I can't have a regular conversation with her. Here's an example. I came home from a weekend conference happy, inspired and full of interesting experiences.

"Five minutes inside the door Cathy said, 'You never called,' in an accusatory voice, no kiss, no 'how was the trip?' I started to explain my cell phone was out of zone, but I couldn't get two words out before she launched into her woes, painting an ugly picture of being alone all weekend. Even though we agreed that I would go to the conference because it's important for my work, I think she resented the fact that I went. Then when she was accusatory, I did feel guilty and responsible for her bad feelings. I think that was her point without her saying it.

"Then her voice reached fever pitch. She said I no longer loved her, I was turned off by her. I was dumbfounded. Not that this sort of thing hasn't happened before but for some reason I wasn't prepared and it made me mad. I started to walk away just to get relief but not before she called me a 'fraidy cat' among other nasty things.

"Isn't that ridiculous? I'm supposed to listen without so much as a 'hi, how are you?' and she has the gall to get upset with me! Everything we talk about gets turned into something else."

**SHORT TERM SOLUTION:** Halt and desist communication. You two are singing a discordant tune together. You blame her; she blames you.

Slow down. Think about the last conversation between the two of you and pinpoint exactly when the first offensive note occurred.

Let her know you cannot listen as long as she can talk. You are not sure why. Then, if you can, agree on a signal that indicates your listening ability is over. Keep the communication problem in your ballpark for now.

Discuss only concrete household issues until you have a plan. Number one on the plan list is to follow through on your goal to remain calm while she talks. Her talking style is intense; it reaches into your emotional centers and escalates feelings and distorts what you are hearing. Calm your mind and listen. If an objective person were standing nearby what would he or she hear?

**LONG TERM SOLUTION:** Altering your listening patterns means concentrating, being conscious of both your style of communicating and reacting as well as your wife's style. What are you doing to exacerbate the situation? The distortion may be your experience, your interpretation or the feelings you generate and she responds to. You have been putting the onus of the problem on your wife.

If you discover that you are doing the twisting, turning and sidestepping you are in luck because you can now change your method of interacting—or not. If your wife is a distorter you can help by listening and responding differently and, therefore, change the way you communicate.

Experiment. Focus totally on Cathy, look at her eyes when you have something to say. Talk softly or loudly. Think about her positive qualities so that the nuances in your face represent pleasure.

But, it is possible that she cannot alter her pattern, that neurons in her brain are set in a particular way, if so, can you cope with her distortion?

**DISTORTION: NOW YOU SEE IT, NOW YOU DON'T**

Melissa's distortion of her husband's personality has reached epidemic proportions and become a serious threat to her husband's standing in his family and in the community. Melissa is determined to establish her husband as mentally ill. She is not saying, as people often do, "That's crazy!" Instead, she is out to prove that her husband is crazy. Step by step she builds her case through magnification and dramatization of behavior and words taken out of context.

Fishing through the internet for definitions, explanations and other people's experiences, Melissa attempts to carefully build a case establishing that her Bill is unstable, diagnosable, using behaviors that fit the DSM IV (Psychiatric Mental Health Manual) category.

With an emotionally disturbed husband Melissa is off the hook. She cannot be blamed for their marital problems. She is healthy, she is acting properly, she is right. He is the problem but, at the same time, he cannot help himself. She is settling in as the long-suffering masochist letting both her family and his know about the pain she is enduring.

Melissa's plan is a solution of sorts. It defines the situation and eases her mind while keeping her locked in an aversive, hostility-filled environment.

## MELISSA & BILL

Bill, 36, a computer and stock market whiz, has insisted on marriage counseling. Melissa, 36, a homemaker, is unhappy about therapy but states that she will help in any way she can. However, she indicates that Bill's mental state is their problem. In their first session Bill relates that his reason for counseling is Melissa's anger toward him.

Melissa says she has to let off steam, "Who wouldn't? Occasionally I get mad, living as I do with a mental case. I build up so much frustration I just blow up—but it only lasts about 10 minutes. That's not much considering what I put up with."

Bill, disagrees, "She doesn't let off steam, she acts crazy: screams, jumps up and down, runs around while she's putting me down. And this is done in front of the children. The woman cannot be contained.

"Melissa is determined to make me crazy or make sure others know I'm seriously off the beam. She has informed every one we know, including my sister, that I have a diagnosable mental illness.

"She denies what I know is a fact. Her attitude does make me crazy. I feel like I've been accused of murder with circumstantial evidence and it's out in the world as a fact. Our families will always wonder, 'Is Bill crazy?' Staying with Melissa makes me wonder myself about my mental health.

"I try to stay away from her now. Anything I say can and will be used against me."

These two are at war. Their problems did not begin when they married, the groundwork had been laid years before. Both came from troubled backgrounds. Melissa's mother criticized her father incessantly. Criticism was such a regular event that Melissa was not aware her mother was being critical. Her parents had no social life because their bickering and harping was impossible for other people to tolerate. Even family members avoided Melissa's parents.

Intellectually Melissa understood her parents' difficulty. Still, Melissa had learned relationship lessons from her parents and internalized the ideal relationship: Attack and grind the other person down. Melissa becomes the powerful mother and Bill, the weak, ineffective father. She is unconsciously working on recreating her parents' marriage.

Bill, who had endured a physically and emotionally abusive parent, did not recognize the beginning of Melissa's abuse. Compared to what he had been through as a child, living with Melissa was a piece of cake. Gradually, though, he realized he felt terrible around his wife, fearful of her moods, and that he doubted himself all over again, just like he did as a child.

Emotionally he tried to protect himself; he withdrew from Melissa. At the same time he began to question his sanity. Bill wanted therapy to either cure himself or put to rest the notion that he was mentally ill. Melissa wanted therapy to prove she was right.

Emotionally, Melissa and Bill are at a preadolescent level and have so much developmental growing to do (if it is going to happen) that improving their life together had not occurred to them.

## MANAGING DISTORTIONS

The distortion in Melissa and Bill's story is obvious but when you live with distortion interpreting the communication style can be difficult. It requires writing, thinking and having serious talks with an objective person.

Once you tease out specific distortion examples you have choices: Stop and alter interactions or acknowledge that crazy making communication will never end.

My suggestions:

1. When you are confused by an interaction, write down exactly what was said. Do not depend on your memory. When you talk to your partner about the conversation you need facts. Without facts you will spin off into another distortion. (This might happen even with facts).
2. Break down the words into fact or distortion. List each fact and list each distortion separately.
3. Tell your wife or husband you want to have a discussion. Set up privacy, exact time of day or night and make the appointment time-limited. When your partner asks, "What is this about?" The subject is communication confusion. Refuse to

enter a discussion at that moment in time; it will not be constructive.

4. Refuse to argue. If one of you refuses to argue, there is no argument.
5. Plan these talks on a regular basis, once a week or twice a month. Be persistent or your partner will not get it. That is, she must know you are serious and through repetition hopefully grasp what you are saying.
6. Your job is to listen carefully and stay on track.
7. Do not be discouraged. Time and energy are required to think through distortion conversation to stay focused.

Illuminate distortion and you unravel communication confusion.

Dissociation is another communication style that produces confusion and unhappiness.

## CHAPTER FOURTEEN

# DISSOCIATION

Three words characterize your life with a dissociator: evaporate, dissipate, and elude. Like a cloud that rolls by, words evaporate and context disappears. Dissociation is child-like. "I didn't do it" or "What are you talking about? I didn't say that." Responsibility for words and behavior is denied; his or her declarations drop through their mind like a sieve.

Dissociate means that, rather than head into the problem, you mentally look the other way and the problem drops out of your mind like it never happened. In pathological cases you take on another personality and are, in effect, a different person.

If your spouse says, "I didn't say that" unless you have recorded his exact words you are stopped dead in your tracks. This conversation is going nowhere.

His reaction does not make sense because, on the one hand, he retains huge amounts of information related to his career performance, stock market indices and basketball, hockey and baseball scores. On the other hand, when it comes to relationship conversations, situations or emotions, his mind is a blank. (You may think that that sentence is a characterization of men's reaction to women's talk—and sometimes it is.)

If your partner uses words or acts in ways that are inappropriate and you are upset, he is puzzled and asks, "What are you talking about?" although he has just stomped around and talked in a loud, chastising voice. You can never pin him down. He will deny saying what he just said and assure you he did not mean it that way.

If you have a problem with his behavior, he is appalled that you are making such a big deal of nothing.

Given his reaction you are shaken, feel invisible and confused.

Dissociation is a short-sighted, shallow, surface life, a state that resembles a person with a lobotomy. (A lobotomy operation electrically shocks particular areas of the brain and clears the memory slate.)

It would be different if he said, "Oh, did I say that? I can't remember." Instead his compartmentalized brain tells him that you are making things up. You are wrong.

A person who compartmentalizes will make a statement and 10 minutes later, an hour later or a day later declare his experience or feelings or ideas are the opposite. When you report feeling puzzled and want clarification a dissociator knows what they have not said and, consequently, cannot alter or give up words or behaviors that are not in his head at that moment in time. In other words he is in a different compartment now and the door on the other compartment clanged shut. He is blank. What are you talking about?

Some would call a dissociator a liar but dissociating indicates conflict, rather than fabrication, a form of compartmentalization. A blatant example is a minister teaching moral values but at the same time embezzling funds.

## MANAGING DISSOCIATION

Larry and Jeannie's remembrances of talks and events always ended with the same frustrating results. Larry said, "Jeannie cannot remember any discussion conclusion regardless of importance. I can't stand it. Even with small things, like a plan to go to the store at 3:30, she will say, 'Oh, I thought you said 4.'

"It's like there's a hole in her head and anything I say drops through and disappears. She's sweet and then suddenly, mean. I don't know what to do. I'm confused. Her behavior feels deliberate, so I want to retaliate and take action. Jeannie is a smart woman but around me she acts brain-dead."

## SOLUTIONS

Here is what you can do. Let your partner know that because she forgets problems and situations, you do not. Talk in a comforting voice and indicate struggles about who said what, when and how are over.

You probably cannot lay the matter to rest when you first discuss the issue so you suggest in a calm, quiet voice that since there is a question about what goes on between you two, perhaps a tape recording or camcorder would solve the dilemma. Buy one and use it.

Do not let the matter drop. Do not get mad. Be persistent. Since she is capable of remembering other situations, have patience and realize that if she recognizes the importance of her forgetfulness with you and wants to change her thought processes, change requires time. Your job is to beam her onto your wavelength by attention to her inattention.

If she chooses not to take you seriously, you change thought patterns, stop frustrated thinking and view interactions as concrete. This is it forever more. You have choices: counseling, acceptance or separation.

Personalization is another personality style that muddies communication waters.

# CHAPTER FIFTEEN

# PERSONALIZATION

To interpret and evaluate individuals from your experience is necessary. To interpret and evaluate others and believe that their words have to do with you when there is no evidence is personalization.

    Everyone has had one of these experiences. You are personalizing when someone across the street laughs and you think that they are laughing at you. When friends are speaking quietly and you cannot hear, they are talking about you. Maybe they are but unless they tell you, your thought is a personalized guess. When your husband is disgruntled, your children disagreeable or your friend snappy, you are somehow responsible. You think, "Uh oh, what did I do?"

    The operative word here is believes. A fleeting thought is simply a thought that comes to mind. Believing your thought is personalization. Personalization is neither rational nor intelligent. It's like looking at a tree and since you cannot see the roots you declare that the tree is a statue.

    Ann is a person who personalizes and that personality trait is jeopardizing her marriage.

## ANN AND KIRK

Casually dressed for her first therapy session, Ann, 34, is an attractive housewife and B.C. (before children) she was a career woman. Kirk, Ann's 36-year-old conservative banker husband, who came to counseling with Ann, reports that he is a home-on-time, no-drinking or carousing kind of guy. He never even considered marijuana as a teenager. In other words, Kirk presents himself as steady as a rock without interest in any extracurricular activities. Ann concurs.

This information is the forerunner of the problem. Ann tells me that she has issues with a neighbor whom she believes Kirk finds attractive.

Ann goes on to say, "Our neighbor, Amanda, is flamboyant and flirtatious and although Kirk assures me he is totally uninterested in Amanda I see an attraction there.

"We were at a neighborhood party where Amanda was dressed in an outfit that looked like a Halloween costume to me or maybe she was just plain trying to be sexy. She had on a very short, tight skirt with a fitted, bodice or something, and she kept talking to Kirk. It made me sick."

Kirk looked distressed and said, "Ann takes as written in stone that her thoughts of seduction are correct. No one is seducing anyone. I don't know where she gets these ideas. Our neighbor dresses like a floozy and she talked to every man at the party."

"Well," Ann said, "What about when I went to pick up Josie (their daughter) at Amanda's house and she thought you were picking up Josie and she had on see through pants?"

Kirk said, "I can't help what she wears, can I?"

Again Ann is back to the idea that Kirk is a co-conspirator, "You answered the phone when she called. She is definitely interested in you. I can tell."

Kirk is beginning to get agitated and raise his voice, "So what? I am not even slightly attracted to or interested in her." Then Kirk turned to me and said, "You can see how we get nowhere. No matter what I say or how I act, Ann is determined she is right.

"She does it about other things, as well. For example, she is dead set on the idea that my father doesn't like her. Ann is a very likeable person. She is normally sweet and nice to people. My dad thinks she's great but she simply won't accept that fact, consequently, she's on edge when he comes over."

Besides the obvious unhappiness personalization causes Kirk, this is where Ann's personalization gets her into trouble. Kirk reported, "One August evening when neighbors were outside chatting Ann made a point of finding Amanda, then in a loud voice proceeded to inform her that she wore slutty clothes, was flirtatious and told her to stop talking to me."

Kirk groaned when he was finished with the story. Kirk said he was furious, embarrassed and totally frustrated. Kirk said, "I told her she is jealous and that made her mad, but the truth is she hasn't been jealous about other women. She just gets weird ideas in her mind and now as a consequence of her behavior I refuse to attend neighborhood parties."

After Kirk's rendition of the confrontation Ann appeared chagrined and half-hearted in her own defense. Nevertheless, she said, "Maybe I was too assertive but I think I needed to confront Amanda. I can't let her get away with chasing my husband."

## PERSONALIZATION SPECIFICS

You cannot help putting your spin on events, but if you do not recognize that these ideas are simply your own point of view, you are bringing everything into your orbit. You are totally subjective; other people's perspectives are either wrong or invalid. You cannot get past yourself when you personalize. Personalization and narcissism are close cousins. When Ann personalizes she:

1. Automatically assumes whatever is going on with Kirk has to do with her.
2. Is what she feels and she feels way too much in reaction to others. She ignores or is missing an intellectual filter. If Kirk is sick, she is sick. Kirk has to dumb down his feelings or monitor what

he says to prevent Ann from taking whatever he says as a personal affront.

3. Projects, which means that she transfers her thoughts to whomever or to Kirk. She thinks to herself, 'He knows I didn't mean that!' and without verbalizing, assumes that that is what Kirk thinks.

Not a pretty picture but, when you know you live with a person who personalizes, you chalk up reactions to a neuron that malfunctions. If you feel the need to confront interactions you can expect an argument indicating that you are wrong. In that case you insist that she has a right to her ideas just as you do. There is a possibility she may acquiesce but in her heart she knows she is right.

**IMMEDIATE SOLUTION:** Stay steady and calm with your version of your truth, which is easier said than done. Arguing will not produce positive results. The issue is how to handle two versions of reality.

**LONG TERM SOLUTION:** We are all defensive at times; we need our defenses. Defenses are meant to protect, not compromise our lives. Half of the communication battle is the ability to see through your defenses even after the fact, so that you can apologize or rehearse giving up a particular defensive behavior or ask your partner to point out when defenses occur. (As I have said before, that might be dangerous unless you are both mature and wise.)

Communication problems that are built into a personality and not the result of developed defenses cannot change. The only change that will ever occur is your recognition that Ann's behavior is written in stone, and it is in your best interest to find a solution that suits you.

1. Your expectations of how Ann should behave or how she should respond sets you up for disappointment, agitation or anger.
2. Approach Ann with the same consideration, kindness and respect that you would give to a stranger. Remain calm.
3. Do not enter into a who-is-right discussion. You are yanking each other down to the lowest common denominator when you struggle with who is right.
4. Instead, take on the role of understanding friend, ally, and co-worker, whichever role feels comfortable. Respectfully listen to her ideas, then insert your own understandings while remaining calm, cool and collected.
5. Your attitude and behavior have a powerful effect on Ann. As difficult as it is, stay steady.

Can you stop frustration that flashes instantaneously into your mind? No. However, the minute you recognize the frustration, let it go. It is an old response that upsets you for no reason. It's the same as stomping your feet like a baby because you want to touch the stove. Stomping your feet gets the baby nowhere, frustration gets you nowhere except distressed. You cannot stop Ann's talk or reactions but you can continue to be rational and in no uncertain terms repeat your point of view.

Ann has self-esteem issues that can be addressed and resolved in therapy—if she is able to absorb ideas that are different than her own. In the meantime because marriage is a seesaw, sooth yourself with the knowledge that in an intimate relationship one person's words and actions have a powerful effect on the other whether the words are immediately acknowledged or not.

## THE PLAN

Tolerance should not have to be forced, and one person should not have to take the role of peacemaker or mediator in a marriage but, in reality, that is often the case. You have to walk the line between giving your partner respect and respecting yourself, but since you chose your partner you are respecting your own choice when you, at the least, use good manners, are polite and friendly. It is in your best interest to bring happiness into your life by taming those resentful, cranky or angry impulses and take the high road.

But, if relationship unhappiness persists, even when you have discovered, defined and found a variety of solutions for difficult specific problems, communication styles or personality characteristics, another avenue is available.

Section Five contains a seven-day, step-by-step plan to shake up "couple habits" and put your relationship on an upward trajectory.

# SECTION FIVE

## THE SEVEN SECRETS OF RELATIONSHIP HAPPINESS

The Seven-Day Action Plan will change your relationship life forever.

# CHAPTER SIXTEEN

# RHODES TO SUCCESS

# RELATIONSHIP HAPPINESS

# SEVEN-DAY PLAN

## SEVEN SECRETS OF RELATIONSHIP HAPPINESS

The seven foundational "secrets" that are essential for a good relationship are not unknown to you. In fact, during your courtship they were your raison d'etre, your life focus, the morning, noon and night love juice flowing through your mind and body. You were doing the right things and didn't even know it.

The secrets are simple: you get what you want when you are crystal clear about your goals and keep your goals in the forefront of your mind.

Your other option is to keep doing what you have done and, of course, you will get what you've gotten to this point—unhappiness. The seven secrets of relationship happiness are a shift from problem-oriented, random, reactionary thoughts and behavior to conscious, determined thoughts and behavior.

When you focus on the secrets of relationship success for (at least) seven days your changed thoughts will be a reflection of what you know is true: to be understood, understand. To be loved, love. What you give to your relationship, you get.

Before you make a decision to follow the seven-day experiment, I would like you to consider the ideas that follow.

## RELATIONSHIPS

Particularly in our first love experience, we overlook any deficiencies in the other person, idealize them, and fantasize an extraordinary relationship—"and we lived happily ever after." Inevitably, the "chemicalized" mind returns to earth and the realities of life intrude. Now we find out if our coping skills will meet the challenges.

In our fantasies relationships and living happily ever after are the same. We meet, electrically connect, move into a love zone and, although we have different backgrounds and experiences, we expect the relationship dance to flow smoothly: No problem-solving experience required.

On the other hand, learning a sport, planning and executing a meal or having a successful relationship requires knowledge, time and effort. Sport proficiency requires practice, making alterations in your stance, changing the way you handle equipment, mental awareness and persistence. Even Tiger Woods, who spent hours as a child practicing his golf swing and is considered one of the greatest golfers of all time, needs assistance from a teaching pro to stay on top of his game. We are no different than Tiger. We need help to let go of old interaction habits and to learn behavior that works.

Happiness and unhappiness are a creation of your 60,000 daily thoughts and feelings.

These thoughts and feelings are often unconscious representations and interpretations creatively selected from parental modeling, individual heredity and history, and the unspoken contract you've established with your partner. Specifics of an actual marital (relationship) contract, other than "richer and poorer, through sickness and health, till death do us part," are usually unspoken.

At the outset of marriage most individuals assume sex, finances and division of household duty among other unexpressed expectations will easily and naturally fall into place. For example, how many people have clearly stated their needs and expectations for sex in their marriage? If one partner assumes that sex will occur four times a week and the other prefers sex once a month someone is going to be disappointed, upset or angry.

It is in your best interest to consciously create happiness for yourself rather than putting your unconscious in charge of your mood and behavior.

## REACTIONS

Here are a few more words of encouragement and tips on how to make sure your plan is fail-proof. When you are following the plan you do not want to be mysterious, act differently and put your partner in the position of wondering what your new behavior means. Present your plan to your partner—and only your partner.

Acknowledge any objections or suggestions offered and say, "thank you". These thoughts belong to your significant other. They do not alter your plan or your goal. If your mate begins a series of questions, doubts, or what-ifs with the implication that your plan cannot work or will be a problem, you will listen, respond as best you can and proceed as planned.

One person in a dyad who thinks and behaves differently produces change.

## PARTNER EXPECTATIONS

Trust your partner to continue his or her same patterns. Your expectations of change have to do with you, only you. The minute you are watching and waiting for acknowledgment that you are different, you are sabotaging your plan. You are the change agent, not your partner.

You are an actor during the seven-day time frame, not a reactor, and as the actor you take charge of yourself and act in ways consistent with your goal. Your partner's words and behavior belong to him even when he says, "Joan, why do you continually do that? What's wrong with you?" Those words belong to him. They are his interpretation. Refuse to absorb them. You do not respond with anger or dismay, instead reply quickly and automatically, "That's an interesting point of view" or "I'll think it over." You refocus and depersonalize as though you are listening to a stranger. If your partner is skeptical or hostile you view that behavior as a challenge. A challenge helps you.

Since relationships have many layers, your seven-day plan calms the first layer and begins to penetrate the next. Keep in mind that any deep-seated difficulty can be tackled after seven days.

## ALTERING HABITS

**Take charge of your mind for seven days with specific goals for each day.** Bore yourself with your plan. Remind yourself of your goals at breakfast, lunch and dinner. Remind yourself of your goals in the car on the way to work, on the way home from work and before you go to sleep. Remind yourself of your goals the moment you wake up in the morning, as you brush your teeth, after lunch and after dinner.

Keep your plan for the day continuously rotating through your mind and remember that concentration and persistence is power. Your motto for yourself is simple: clear, direct thoughts as well as simple, clear, direct communication.

Every word you communicate to your partner will be positive for seven days. Each day is a day of positive thoughts and a day of conscious release of habitual unhappy thoughts and feelings. You are bringing together your mental, physical and emotional strength with one goal in mind: self-management. Initially you may gag on all the positive talk to yourself but stay steady with your plan and do not deviate regardless of rebuttals, doubt, fear or any other reactions from your significant other and especially from yourself.


## STAY ON TARGET

When you say to yourself, "I cannot stay 'unnaturally' conscious 24/7," I say, "Yes, you can." Your problem-solving methods have not made you happy. This is you taking charge and changing the nature of your relationship.

When you say to yourself, "I'm sick of this. I am not doing this any more." Yes, you are. Remember your unhappiness.

When you say to yourself, "He is not doing anything." That's right. So what? Stop whining.

For seven days you robotically, faithfully follow the seven secrets of relationship happiness project that follow:

1. Speak positively
2. Think positively
3. Positive emotions
4. Compliment your partner
5. Develop listening skills
6. Forgive the past
7. Generate solutions

## COMMUNICATE POSITIVELY AND CLEARLY

### DAY 1   SPEAK POSITIVELY

On day one every word you speak to your partner is positive. Speak about what you like. Show appreciation. Put sticky notes in your car, on your desk or wherever you spend your daytime and nighttime to remind yourself to speak positively. Speak and act in a loving, positive manner toward your mate.

Communication confusion often results from discrepancies between the message sent and the message received. When your spouse speaks your job is to ask for clarification and acknowledge his or her thought and feeling. If your partner says something that surprises or puzzles you, instead of supplying your own meaning, ask for clarification. Ask questions without voice inflections that suggest you know better.

Mirror what you hear your partner saying in a positive tone and upbeat manner. Resist giving advice and do not verbalize your interpretation or assume the worst. Reflect both the content and feeling of your partner's words as though you are translating a foreign language. Your translation may feel or sound awkward, don't let that stop you. The goal is to clarify in a pleasant, positive manner.

The second you begin to react by bickering, arguing, defending yourself or disputing your partner's words, stop it! It wasn't effective in the past and it won't be effective at this moment in time. Find some truth in his or her words regardless of whether the content seems wrong or ridiculous to you.

Eliminate hostility from your conversation. If your partner points out that you seem angry, hostile or sarcastic, do not put on an innocent act or feel that you have to rebut the statement. Take it like a grown up and thank him for his observation (no matter what thought or feeling you have).

Use your mate's observations to help you. We cannot see or hear ourselves objectively. You may be presenting yourself in a manner that is not in your best interest.

Whatever your partner says or feels belongs to him. During this seven-day period you do not personalize his thoughts or feelings. You depersonalize as though you are listening to a stranger.

Inner negative dialogue will sway attention from your goal and your resolve will waver. Simply replace negative dialogue with positive dialogue. Remind yourself that this is a seven-day project and you can do anything for seven days. Do not let yourself down.

Focus on positive behavior. Congratulate yourself.

## DAY 2        THINK POSITIVELY

Life reflects your positive thought choice. Happiness within is reflected by happiness without.

Think about what you are thinking about. You have an ongoing dialogue in your mind that you can control; you can think anything you want to think. This minute think about the positive experience you want in your relationship.

Squelch any negative thoughts, no matter how real they seem or how important it seems to express the thoughts. For example, "I'm doing all the changing here, she is doing nothing." Yes, you are changing and that means you have control of yourself. "She always reacts like that—that makes me mad!" You are in charge of your thought processes. No other person can make you mad.

When you catch yourself thinking negatively, stop. Think again. Replace a negative idea immediately with love or, if you can't muster love thoughts, any neutral, positive thought will do.

Expect old thoughts to pop into your mind. Do not speak about the past. It's over. Discussing it one more time won't change anything.

Do not mentally editorialize by saying to yourself, "Can't be done. There he goes again. It's hopeless. This won't work." Negative, judgmental thoughts sabotage your goal. They are old, fragmented thoughts that will be real if you make them real.

CALM DOWN. STOP NEGATIVE DIALOGUE.

Maximize opportunities to stay on target with your happiness goals. At the same time be aware that at times you will regress and oppositional thoughts will surface. When old thoughts and feelings enter your mind, take a deep breath and bring focused consciousness to your goal for the day. Historical negative thoughts and agitated feelings will disappear when you take charge of yourself and deliberately let them go—new thoughts may last for only a moment and old worry, agitation or negative thoughts may slip back into place. Catch the negative thought and tell yourself it is historical, it is not real.

You have been communicating your entire life and have developed thought pathways in your brain that may not be positive and solution oriented. Be patient with yourself and your partner. You are in an experimental time capsule. Right now you are a robot following instructions.

What is real at this moment in time is your goal to take charge of your thoughts. You are focused on thinking and speaking positively rather than reacting to thoughts that come to mind.

You handled your thoughts today and made sure they were upbeat. If not, note what went wrong and rehearse ideal thoughts and words.

## DAY 3        POSITIVE FEELINGS

Cement these thoughts in place: You feel great today. You are happy that you are a thinking person who has decided to improve life by changing thoughts and speaking positively. You can handle anything that comes your way because you are relaxed, you feel good and you are going to make sure you continue to feel good all day and all night. The thoughts you think and the words you speak are uplifting to you and everyone around you.

Feelings are fueled by thoughts. You rely on feelings to feed yourself-information. At any moment a thinking glitch may occur and you are switched onto an old, negative dialogue path with feelings of depression, anxiety, anger or any number of sad, sorrowful feelings. No problem.

Catch the thoughts as quickly as you can, stop your mind, and replace negative with positive feelings immediately.

When you are feeling uneasy and unhappy you rummage around until you dredge up a reason: "I think the marriage is falling apart. I hate the way George talks to me" or "I'm afraid she might leave in spite of all I'm doing." Will those feelings and dialogue help you? No.

Instead, acknowledge the feeling and deliberately let it go with a command to yourself that you are not going to feel sad or bad at this moment. Put the feeling in an imaginary bag and imagine throwing it into the garbage.

Conversely, it's important to express feelings openly and freely. Feelings are a part of the human experience. Because they come to mind does not mean you: 1) Entertain them; 2) Use them as an excuse to pout, withdraw or act aggressively; or, 3) Indicate you know how your spouse feels and you feel 10 times worse.

I am not suggesting you bottle yourself up forever. It is important to be authentic. If you feel angry with your mate for present or past words or behavior, get out pen and paper or use your computer to express negative feelings and move those feelings out of your system (and do not leave that information lying around). Your job at this moment in time is to focus on positive thoughts and behavior and eliminate depressed negative feelings.

Take charge when you feel tense or nervous and the feeling will go away. Shake it out by exercising. Any form of exercise for an hour will eliminate stressed feelings.

And do not moan about the time it takes to exercise. We find time to do whatever is a priority. You know tension and nervousness affect your relationship; you are self-absorbed when you feel miserable.

Do not be discouraged! This is an experiment and experiments take time and focused attention. Every hour on the hour tell yourself how energized and positive you feel. Rome wasn't built in a day and neither was your relationship.

## DAY 4          COMPLIMENT YOUR PARTNER

Today, once every hour, take just one minute to think of one specific positive attribute of your partner: physical and/or intellectual attributes, mothering or fathering skills, things s/he does for you. Then speak about those qualities and be specific. For example, instead of "You are a good father," say, "When I hear you talking to Johnny about his skate boarding, he lights right up. I can feel the love and respect between you."

To compliment sincerely is giving a gift to yourself. You feed your soul when you think and speak of others in ways that uplift their spirit.

If complimenting your partner feels awkward or insincere, your job is to overcome the feeling. Stay on target. If you do not feel like complimenting your partner, tell yourself, "So what?" Often you are caught in traffic and are frustrated. So what? You are still caught in traffic.

At first you may struggle to present the compliment or even get it out of your mouth. On top of your discomfort you may have to deal with your partner's surprise, discomfort, disbelief or questioning tone.

If your spouse enjoyed the compliment that's great! If not, your job is not to dissect or evaluate your partner's reply. You will know a bull's eye compliment when it occurs. Like anything, the more experience you have the better you will do.

How many times did you compliment your partner? One compliment is oil in the machinery of your relationship. Tomorrow add to your compliment score.

Compliments are positive. Your job is to think, feel and act positively. Remind yourself with sticky notes.

## DAY 5      LISTENING SKILLS: ACKNOWLEDGE YOUR PARTNER'S WORDS AND FEELINGS

Consciously relax your mind and body. Prepare to eliminate any negative, judgmental thoughts that come to mind.

Today you will spend 10 concurrent minutes (at least) focused on your partner, listening, seriously noting what he is saying and thoughtfully responding. Put yourself in his shoes. No uh huh or um's.

Today you understand whatever your partner says; you understand that his words have to do with his understanding of the world. Even if the words are addressed to you or are about you, they belong to your mate. The words may or may not be relevant. Setting your spouse straight is irrelevant.

Depersonalize. Whatever he communicates to you through body language or words has to do only with your partner. If you are having an emotional reaction or have a powerful need to express an opposite opinion, a denial or simply a different point of view, write it down and wait for ten days. After 10 days if you still need expression you will share your opinion at that time.

Your job is to rephrase what your partner says and indicate you are paying attention. You are interested in the manner in which his mind works.

If your partner lets you know you misunderstood, fine. It is possible that you are unconsciously editing his opinion. Thank your mate. View misunderstandings as educational.

You are willing, eager and available to listen. Pretend you are talking to a stranger who speaks peculiarly and softly. You have to really pay attention to understand. You are open, nonjudgmental, accepting, compassionate, and cooperative.

Your hearing system is finely tuned.

## DAY 6        FORGIVE AND FORGET THE PAST

Day six is forgiveness day. Forgive your misdeeds as well as your mate's; let the past go. You cannot relive them and, more importantly, educating your signifcant other by dredging up historical miseries is like spitting in the wind.

You may say to yourself, "She said I am stupid, she embarrassed me in front of my boss,  and once slapped my face. I'll never be able to forgive her for those insults." However, if you don't learn to forgive and move on, you have created your own emotional prison.

Your choice is to make both of you miserable by keeping the past alive or, instead, use hurts as learning tools. Lance Armstrong, the seven-time winner of the Tour de France, credits his testicular cancer with his success. He took the challenge and overcame it. Your goal is to turn away from the blame game, put aside the bitterness and retribution, and forgive.

Consciously dedicate this day as a day to replace ugly, mean-spirited thoughts about the past with a mind-set that is first calm, then satisfied, and finally one that brings happiness. When you realize that everything is fundamentally a matter of perception, and that you can control your mind, you go from resentment to forgiveness.

Remember—when distressing incidents occurred in the past you and your partner were different people. At a later time, if you cannot let go of an incident from the past you will take the information to a psychologist and therapeutically work it out.

Dismiss and forgive historical negative thoughts, words and behaviors.

## DAY 7    GENERATE SOLUTIONS

Today move into a concrete business mind-set orientation. If a problem arises and it must be solved during this seven-day time frame creatively generate several possible solutions and ask your partner to do the same.

You have good ideas but you do not know best. Be willing to be wrong. Cooperate. Look for peaceful, mediated solutions, which means both your ideas and your partner's are considered.

Generating solutions requires a business mind-set.

1. Determine ahead of time that the discussion will be calm, cool and collected. If either of you becomes agitated, call time out and resume later.
2. Assign a specific time to talk about the problem and talk only about the problem at that time.
3. Stop talking when twenty minutes has passed no matter where you are in the solution process.
4. At the end of 20 minutes, write down the solutions you have reached and schedule another meeting.
5. Listen carefully. No interruptions.

You are presenting possibilities. If your solution is batted down, pout for a second then move on. No quips such as, "Well, you have such great ideas. I don't notice you solving the problem." Do not verbalize this type of thinking. You simply let it pass through your mind.

Every problem has a solution.

## ADDITIONAL IDEAS

### PRACTICE

During your seven-day project keep reminding yourself to stay in the conscious programming. Practice, practice, practice. Don't let your mind drift off into mental mayhem. Concentrate your energy on positively changing thoughts and feelings.

Plan on feeling resistance not only from your partner, but also from yourself. When you hear thoughts that are in opposition to your stated goal, clear them out. Be prepared for your mind to fragment. Expect habit-driven mental configurations to segue into worry, doubt, anxiety, depression, fearfulness. Resistant new thoughts may jump into mind to dismiss and discount the seven secrets.

View your mind as a computer by deleting all thoughts and feelings that sabotage positive seven-day goals. The worst mistake you can make now is to relax into old habits.

### MISLEADING BEHAVIOR

If you think that you do not want to mislead your spouse by acting positively when you actually have thoughts that the relationship may not work or separation may be in the future, remember your partner is grown up. You are not responsible for his behavior. He will react in whatever manner is right for him.

The fact is that you are in the relationship right now. It does not make sense that you have to be distant or negative to protect your spouse from disappointment just in case the relationship ultimately does not work.

If you are cheerful and positive you feel better and people around you feel better. If you do ultimately separate, you are making a future relationship amicable by starting now and putting your best foot forward.

## WHAT IF NOTHING IN THE RELATIONSHIP CHANGES?

At the end of seven days the worst that can happen is that you will be disappointed, feel sad, feel angry, feel pain; you will feel what you have felt before. Even disappointment is helpful. It helps clarify what is and is not possible.

Your relationship is like a heart condition, wherever you go and whatever you do you are never free; the rhythmic, soothing beat or the erratic, angry beat of the relationship affects every part of your life.

Now you see that you have options: You can either stay the same, continue to enhance the partnership or realize that it's time to stop the struggle and move on in your life.

You choose.

## BIBLIOGRAPHY

Gottman, John. 1994. *Why Marriages Succeed or Fail.* Simon & Schuster. New York.

Howard, Pierce J.. 2000. *The Owner's Manual for the Brain.* Bard Press. Austin, Texas.

Lamanna, Mary Ann & Riedmann, Agnes. 1994. *Marriages & Families.* Wadsworth Publishing Co., Belmont CA.

McGraw, Phillip C. 2000. *Relationship Rescue.* Hyperion, N.Y.

McKay, Matthew, Fanning, Patrick & Paleg, Kim. 1994. *Couple Skills.* Barnes & Noble, New York.

Rhodes, Carol L. & Norman S. Goldner. 1993. *Why Women and Men Don't Get Along.* Somerset Publishing: Troy, MI.

Rhodes, Carol L. 2000. *Affairs: Emergency Tactics.* Somerset Publishing: Troy, MI.

Schwartz, Jeffrey M., M.D., and Begley, Sharon. 2002. *The Mind and the Brain.* HarperCollins Publishers Inc: New York, N.Y.

Seligman, Martin E. P. 2002. *Authentic Happiness.* Free Press, A Division of Simon & Schuster, Inc., New York, N.Y.

Skolnick, Irene S. 1987. *The Intimate Environment.* Little, Brown & Co., Boston.

Steinmetz, Suzanne, Sylvia Claven and Karen F. Stein. *Marriage & Family Realities*. 1990. Harper & Row Publishers, N.Y.

Strong, Bryan and Christine DeVault. 1992. *The Marriage & Family Experience*. West Publishing Co., St. Paul, MN.

Time-Life Books (1991). *The Mystifying Mind*. Alexandria, VA.